Daoist Sexual Arts

Daoist Sexual Arts

A Guide for Attaining Health, Youthfulness, Vitality, and Awakening the Spirit

Translation and Commentary
by Stuart Alve Olson

Edited by Patrick D. Gross

Valley Spirit Arts
Phoenix, Arizona

Copyright © 2015 by Stuart Alve Olson.
All rights reserved. No part of this book may be reproduced or used in any form or by any means, electronic or mechanical, including photocopying, recording, or by any information storage and retrieval system, without prior written permission from Stuart Alve Olson and Valley Spirit Arts.

Library of Congress Control Number: 2015904269

ISBN-13: 978-1-5088-9168-0
ISBN-10: 1-5088-9168-0

Valley Spirit Arts, LLC
www.valleyspiritarts.com
contact@valleyspiritarts.com

Acknowledgments

With great gratitude, I thank Master T.T. Liang for opening the door to me concerning these Daoist sexual teachings and internal alchemy practices. His pragmatic insights have served me well during the writing of this book and others.

Special thanks to the late Lin Yaoguan who provided me with so much knowledge and documents on the sexual practices. May your crane fly you back as quickly as possible.

To Ms. Song Guan who so generously provided me with several Chinese texts on sexual teachings.

Much appreciation to my wife, Lily, who put forth great effort in the content editing of the first draft of this book and provided me with many wonderful insights on feminine sexual issues and functions.

Finally, to Patrick Gross, who made this book a reality by editing, typesetting, and designing it. My deepest appreciation for all his hard work.

The Intercourse Between the Dragon and Tiger

The white faced boy rides upon the White Tiger.
The green robed girl bestrides the Green Dragon
When the lead and mercury unite in the cauldron,
instantly they are then congealed together.

From the Ming dynasty print of the
Jade Tablet Decree on Nature and Life (性命圭旨, *Xing Ming Gui Zhi*)

Contents

Preface 1
Brief Biographies of the Two Attributed Authors 7
Introduction 15

Book One
The Immortaless He Xiangu
on the Correct Course for Female Practice

He Xiangu's Introduction 29
Chapter One: Laying the Foundation and Purifying the Heart 41
Chapter Two: Cultivating the Menses 47
Chapter Three: Slaying the Dragon 51
Chapter Four: Restore the Breasts to Youthfulness 55
Chapter Five: Establishing the Crucible and Creating the Fetus 59
Chapter Six: Self-Regulate Embryonic Breathing 61
Chapter Seven: Return the Fluid to Form the Fetus 65
Chapter Eight: Refining and Transforming the Yang Spirit 69
Chapter Nine: Perfect and Illuminate the Yang Spirit 73
Chapter Ten: Nourish the Yang Spirit 77

Book Two
The Immortal Zhang Sanfeng's Summary on Gathering the True Root-Power

Part One: The Nine Fundamentals for Gathering the True Root-Power

Laying the Foundation 85
  Fundamental One: Gathering the Medicine 87
  Fundamental Two: Knowing the Correct Time 91
  Fundamental Three: Strumming the Zither 93
  Fundamental Four: Approaching the Opposition 95
  Fundamental Five: Inverting 99
  Fundamental Six: Utmost Sincerity 101
  Fundamental Seven: The River Cart 105
  Fundamental Eight: A Seal on the Gate 109
  Fundamental Nine: Be With and Against the Natural Course 113
Summary of the Nine Fundamentals 115

Part Two: The Seventeen Counsels on Gathering the True Root-Power

Counsel One: Strumming the Zither 119
Counsel Two: Dragon and Tigress Intertwine 121
Counsel Three: Producing Fire, Stimulating Water 123
Counsel Four: Green Dragon, Black Turtle 125
Counsel Five: The Dragon Appears to Seize the Tigress 127
Counsel Six: Dragon Enters the Tigress's Lair 129
Counsel Seven: True Lead Arrives 131
Counsel Eight: Eastern Road Opens 133

Counsel Nine: Push and Pull the Wei Lu 135

Counsel Ten: The Doors of Qian and Kun 137

Counsel Eleven: The River Cart 141

Counsel Twelve: The Multistoried Pavilion 145

Counsel Thirteen: Chun and Meng 149

Counsel Fourteen: Seek the Jade Flowers 151

Counsel Fifteen: Obtain the Yellow Gold 153

Counsel Sixteen: Advancing Yang, Converging Yin 155

Counsel Seventeen: The True Lead of Immortality 159

Appendix

Individual Practice Regimes for Restoration, Developing Jing, Accumulating Qi, and Illumining the Spirit 165

The Nine Sexual Intercourse Positions 171

The Eight Benefits of Sexual Intercourse 179

The Three Oral Treasures 185

The Jade Pool Effect 193

Preface

Before venturing into the explanations of Daoist sexual arts, readers must first understand that the two main texts presented in this work are a combination of sexual health practices and Daoist internal alchemy, which cannot be separated. Daoism views sex as spiritual, so the very act of having sex is transcendental. Readers, especially those not acquainted with Daoist philosophy and practice, may find some of the words strange and even unintelligible. I have tried my best to make the more mystical terms and ideas clear. Internal alchemy is really not all that difficult in practice, but it can be confusing in the study of these texts. I hope this aspect does not deter the reader from thoroughly examining the advice given in these works, as they are truly effective and, more so, mind expanding, especially concerning the use, function, and possibilities of sex.

With that said, I advise readers to review the entire work, as some of the necessary information and explanations do not occur until later in the work. There is simply too much information to absorb on any given subject at the first mention of it.

The material in this book comes from two main sources: a treatise written exclusively for females on sexual restoration/transformation that is attributed to the Daoist immortaless He Xiangu (何仙姑) and a treatise on the sexual practices for sexual restoration/transformation for males and couples, attributed to the immortal Zhang Sanfeng (張三豐).

These two documents, in my opinion, well represent the teachings on Daoist sexual practices. I have also supplemented this work with information from documents stemming from the schools of Joining Vital Energies (合氣派, He Qi Pai), Taboo Girl (某女教, Mou Nu Jiao), White Tiger Green Dragon (白虎青龍派, Bai Hu Qing Long Pai), and from the *Plain Girl Classic* (素女經, *Su Nu Jing*).

These additional writings were necessary to include because the two main texts frequently allude to certain regimes and teachings required for experiencing the ideal outcomes of various sexual practices without going into detail about them. They assume too much knowledge on the reader's part, a common problem with texts such as these. Keep in mind that these treatises were not written for public dissemination but for knowledgeable students of their particular sect.

Including these explanations, however, requires a greater explicitness on sexual themes and activity. For Western readers to really apply and understand these teachings, such explicit and direct language is necessary, but this means foregoing the customary Chinese approach toward discussions of a sexual nature, which are cloaked in subtler terms and what I call "Chinese sensibilities" on sexual matters.

Throughout this work, the term "Dragon" is used for males, and "Tigress" for females. Although the texts make frequent use of *Dragon* and *Tiger* to mean "male" and "female," the Tiger is the metaphor for females, so it seemed more appropriate to translate it with a feminine context as "Tigress" instead.

One important issue must be addressed before the reader plunges into this work, and that concerns the use of multiple sexual partners, which was assumed in these Chinese (both Daoist and Confucian) works on bedchamber sexual practices and arts. This book is neither condoning nor promoting the use of multiple sexual partners, rather it is more directed at how

Preface

Harmonizing the Male and Female Essences
男 女 精 協 和

If the image of Kan [坎, Water, ☵] is over filled, then Li [離, Fire, ☲] completes Qian [乾, Heaven, ☰]. The positions of Heaven and Earth [坤, Kun, ☷] are then established. The origin is restored and it returns to the source.

From the Jade Tablet Decree on Nature and Life

> These verses are saying that when the feminine (Kan) becomes filled (replenished) with the water element (the saliva, sexual secretions, blood, and marrow) this will complete the male, the Fire (Li) element (the Qi and breath), and so becomes pure Yang (Heaven/Qian, the Yanq spirit). When this occurs, the male (Heaven, Yang) and female (Earth, Yin) are then positioned in their proper places and are in harmony. When harmonious, their origin (Before Heaven/prenatal/innate) condition is restored and so one can enter the Dao (Returning to the Source).

self-cultivators and couples may make use of these teachings for the betterment of their physical and relationship health.

There are two streams of thought on the use of multiple partners in Chinese sexual arts. The first is that of the Confucianists. Since only biological immortality (the production of male sons to continue a blood line) mattered to them, women were of less concern in the restoration and spiritual aspects of sexuality. The benefits of such practices were reserved solely for males, hence the use of multiple young women for their sexual dalliances was commonplace. This practice is normally referred to as Grafting (採捕, Cai Bu). Literally meaning to "collect and capture," Grafting is specifically about the taking of female essences and energy, also known as "using the Yin to replenish the Yang." In Daoism, the idea of Grafting was considered injurious (physically and mentally) because true cultivation of sexual energy required the harmonization of both the male and female, which they called Joining Vital Energies (合氣, He Qi).

In Daoist sexual practices, males indeed applied "using the Yin to replenish the Yang," but they balanced this with the idea of females "using the Yang to replenish the Yin." In brief, Joining Vital Energies meant just that—the "joining and harmonizing" of Yin Qi (female energy) and Yang Qi (male energy) into one whole, wherein the energies of both were heightened, increased, and harmonized for purposes of physical restoration and spiritual transformation of everyone.

Within the texts of this work, there does exist the implications of using multiple sexual partners. In the case of He Xiangu's treatise, for example, she advises females not to abide by convention, meaning the normal adherence to the ideal of marriage and monogamy, a social and religious pressure put on

Preface

most women. She viewed these as detrimental to attaining the goal of becoming an immortaless, as it is viewed that one male is incapable of providing the necessary energy needed for her purposes.

In Zhang Sanfeng's treatises, there is mention of having two or three females for sexual practice, but only in context for the purposes of maintaining a consistent practice period wherein the menstrual cycle of one female would not interrupt the male's ongoing daily practice. In both these cases, the underlying use of multiple sexual partners is not in keeping with the intents of Grafting.

Again, however, this work is not implying that multiple partners are necessary or required, as much can be accomplished through monogamist and self-stimulation practice, and since the information given is equally pointed at internal alchemy, a great deal can be accomplished through auto-sexual adherence.

In the end, this work is about using and enhancing sexual energy (whether one practices alone, with a partner, or with multiple sexual partners) to develop a person's health, youthfulness, longevity, and the more lofty goal of immortalizing and awakening the spirit.[1]

---

1   For more information on this subject, see *Being Daoist: The Way of Drifting with the Current* by Stuart Alve Olson (Valley Spirit Arts, 2015).

Brief Biographies of the Two Attributed Authors

He Xiangu
何仙姑

Her name translates as "Immortaless He" and she lived during the Tang dynasty (618–907 CE) He Xiangu is the only female member of the famous folklore group the "Eight Immortals." Lu Dongbin (a major figure in the Eight Immortals) is thought to have given her a peach of immortality.

According to legend, He Xiangu was a native of Guangdong province. At birth, she had six long hairs on the crown of her head, a sign of a sage. When she was around fourteen years old a divine personage appeared to her in a dream (Lu Dongbin) and instructed her to eat a peach, or in some accounts, powdered mica, so her body might become etherealized and immortal. She swallowed it and immediately could fly in the clouds.

She was known to go up and down mountains as if she had wings. Every day at dawn she would leave and return at dusk with baskets full of mountain fruits she had gathered. Gradually, she gave up eating ordinary foods and practiced living off Wind (the breath) and Dew (the saliva).

After her mother passed away when she was still an adolescent, she was forced to become a servant girl. She suffered a great deal of abuse by her owner, which may have been why Lu Dongbin, out of compassion, had saved her.

Later, the Empress Wu dispatched a messenger to summon her to the palace, but on the way there, she disappeared.

Sometime during the Jing Long period (about 707 CE), she ascended to an immortal paradise in broad daylight, becoming a Daoist immortal and joining the group of Eight Immortals. She is usually depicted as a beautiful young maiden carrying a bamboo flute or ladle and holding a peach and lotus flower.

After Lu Dongbin had saved her, she immediately vowed to never marry or bear children (probably so they couldn't suffer the same abuses that she did). Some accounts assume from this vow that she maintained celibacy, but she didn't vow to not have sex. She did not promote monogamy nor the rejection of being sexual, rather she rejected the ideas of marriage and monogamy. Because of her beliefs she figures heavily in the manuals of the bedchamber arts (such as in the first text presented in this book).

She is also traditionally considered a spiritual patron of females in China, who would attempt to invoke her for spiritual wisdom and protection, for bestowing an auspicious blessing of an immortal visitation upon them, and for being blessed with good husbands and lovers. Her depiction with a peach is interesting because this associates her with Xi Wangmu,[1] the

Brief Biographies of the Two Attributed Authors

matriarch of sexual alchemy. The bamboo flute is a symbolic representation of the penis in Daoism, and the lotus flower is an expression of both wisdom and the vagina. So, on one hand, her association with the sexual arts is clear, but on the other hand, when considering her life story, her connection seems obscure as her biographies never actually depict her as being sexual with anyone, only that she vowed to never marry or practice monogamy.

The section in this book attributed to He Xiangu consists of ten methods, or theorems, for females, with the goal of addressing specific feminine issues of sexual-spiritual cultivation. Namely, the reduction and regulation of the menses and for developing the Yang spirit.

Females injure their essence (Jing) by excessive dissipation caused through the menstrual flow (as males do by excessive dissipation of their semen), and so the methods taught here are about bringing a female back to the youthful condition of before she experienced her menstrual flow or to the condition of when she first began menstruating. The emphasis of He Xiangu's work, however, is on strengthening the Yang spirit that often remains dormant in females. Women are Yin by nature, but to achieve balance and harmony, they must seek to develop their Yang spirit, just as men, predominantly Yang in nature, need to develop their Yin spirit.

When a female reduces and regulates her menstrual flow and produces her Yang spirit, she is developing her essence (Jing) so that her Qi and spirit (Shen) will produce the necessary energies for achieving health, beauty, and longevity, and ultimately the state of an immortaless as well.

Daoist Sexual Arts

Zhang Sanfeng
張三豐

No one knows with absolute authority that Zhang Sanfeng was an actual person, but evidence in Chinese history does suggest he existed. He is the attributed founder of Taijiquan (Tai Chi Chuan) and author of several works on Daoist internal alchemy practices, including the second section of this book.

Zhang reportedly lived from 1247 CE to 1417 CE, spanning the Yuan, Ming, and Qing dynasties. Whether he was an actual person or not is irrelevant as the works attributed to him are without doubt some of the most influential works in Daoism, and within Chinese culture itself. Zhang Sanfeng embodied the ideal character of a Daoist immortal, both as a scholar and wanderer. The Wu Dang sect (from Wu Dang Mountain) upholds him as the founder of its teachings, and the Quan Zhen sect, headquartered in Beijing at White Cloud Monastery, enshrined him as a True Immortal Ancestor of Daoism.

One of the more curious stories about Zhang Sanfeng is his meeting with his primary teacher, Fire Dragon Immortal, on Ge Hong Mountain when he was seventy-eight years old.[2] With the

Brief Biographies of the Two Attributed Authors

Fire Dragon Immortal (whom Zhang refers to in his section of this book as "My late teacher") he reportedly learned the three entrances of Daoist cultivation for attaining immortality—*Awakening the Spiritual Nature, Nourishing-Life,* and *Harmonizing the Yin and Yang*. It is the third entrance (Harmonizing the Yin and Yang) that concerns the use of sexual energy and practices for furthering the process of becoming immortal. His teacher, after teaching him for several years, sent Zhang away, claiming that he needed to go to another sacred mountain to practice and attain immortality.

Zhang ended up on Wu Dang Mountain and lived in a remote hut. Rumors circulated that he had brought with him two female disciples with whom he practiced the Harmonizing Yin and Yang teachings. The history of Zhang Sanfeng on Wu Dang Mountain has so many variations, however, that it is near impossible to state any story with accuracy. Supposedly while living there, he created Taijiquan, attained immortality, taught numerous other students, and laid the ground work for the now famous Wu Dang Temple. He is also said to have written several treatises (such as the one presented in this book).

In the end, little is known of what Zhang actually wrote. All we have are several treatises attributed to him, and of these, his *Taijiquan Treatise, Essays on the Essentials of the Great Dao, Refining the Elixir,*[3] and *Gathering the True Root-Power* (translated herein) are of the greatest importance.

The first part of *Gathering the True Root-Power* outlines nine fundamentals for the practice of sexual alchemy. The second part, consisting of seventeen counsels, provides deeper explanations of the nine fundamentals. None of these are progressive teachings. They represent a summary and explanation of the main points of the philosophy and practice, thus giving readers the option to work on whatever fundamental or counsel they wish.

Concluding Remarks

Because of the depth of information presented in the two main texts, it is best, in my opinion, to focus on just one or a few of the practices at a time. Taken in their entirety, these teachings are daunting. I say this because they are a mixture of health and longevity methods, sexual practices, and internal alchemy teachings all rolled into one, and it takes time to absorb what is useful and positive to readers and potential practicers of these sexual methods in present times.

Although these theories are easy to contemplate and study, the actual application and practice of them is quite another thing. My hope, though, is that readers will discover many new insights on the integration of sexuality and spirituality. To that end, I believe, this work is quite important for cultivators of the Way.

Brief Biographies of the Two Attributed Authors

1   Xi Wangmu (西王母), Western Royal Mother, is considered the spiritual matriarch of Daoism. She and three of her four female attendants—Plain Girl, Mysterious Girl, and Multihued Girl (shown in the following illustration, along with Taboo Girl, her fourth attendant)—taught Huang Di (黃帝), the Yellow Emperor (circa 2800 BCE), the methods of sexual internal alchemy, as found in the works of the *Internal Medicine Classic* (內經, *Nei Jing*) and the *Plain Girl Classic* (素女, *Su Nu Jing*).

2   For more information on the history of Zhang Sanfeng, see *Tai Ji Quan Treatise: Attributed to the Song Dynasty Daoist Priest Zhang Sanfeng, Daoist Immortal Three Peaks Zhang Series* (Valley Spirit Arts, 2011).

3   See the forthcoming book, *Refining the Elixir: The Internal Alchemy Teachings of Daoist Immortal Zhang Sanfeng* (Daoist Immortal Three Peaks Zhang Series).

Introduction

Daoist Sexual Arts

Whether one engages in sexual activity for procreation, recreation, restoration, or transformation, the notion that our regenerative energy is intrinsically bound to our spiritual nature is rarely discussed. Sex is, without question, the most powerful of all energies in the human psyche. No other force within us can drive us to such heights of love or to the lowest depths of depravity. Sexual abandon and lust can greatly injure one's body and mind, yet focused and loving sex can produce an almost miraculous healing of afflictions. The purpose for engaging in Daoist sexual practices is for restoring one's regenerative energy (Jing) and vitality (Qi), a means by which to increase one's health and longevity, and as a basis for engaging in the internal alchemy practices leading to the immortalization of one's spirit (Shen).[1]

The teachings reveal ways to recapture the energy, sensitivity to sensations, and intensity of experiences people had as they transitioned from puberty to sexual maturity.

Just as a teenager undergoes tremendous physical and psychological changes from childhood to adulthood, so does a cultivator when transforming spiritually from mortality to immortality. To accomplish this spiritual transformation, the Daoist seeks to recapture his or her youthful regenerative energy so it can be directed toward attaining the experience of Spirit Illumination.[2]

The principles of internal alchemy in Daoism include both sexual and non-sexual practices. Some teachers promote celibacy and others, sexual stimulation—and some a combination of the two. For example, in the teachings of Li Qingyun, the 250-year-old man,[3] he advised students to be sexual during the spring and summer months, but celibate during the autumn and winter months, essentially following nature itself. Other teachings promote the idea of having sexual encounters only on the auspicious days of a month, or even during certain hours within a day. Then there are teachings that instruct restricting sexual release to a certain number of times each week or month.

Daoism doesn't necessarily favor one path or teaching over another. Typically, Daoists teach a combination of both periods of celibacy and activity, carefully balancing sexual activity to further the spiritual transformation of an individual. People often question which approach is more effective, but there is no set answer, as it really is a matter of what works best for each person.

For those who have been led to believe that celibacy is more spiritual than sexual practices, the following quote from the book *The Secret and Sublime* by John Blofeld clarifies the Daoist perspective on the matter:

> I wish only that you had the breadth of vision to perceive that the path of the green dragon and white tiger[4] and the path of chastity run parallel. Those who engage in dual cultivation [sexual practices][5] with deep sincerity are no less pure in heart than lifelong celibates, for both have abandoned the trivial preoccupations of worldly men to seek an exalted goal.
>
> —The Abbot of the Cloud Valley Hermitage

Celibacy is no more a guarantee of spiritual progress than is engaging in sexual practices. Celibacy in some can lead to fanaticism, and sometimes health problems, especially liver and

Introduction

intestinal dysfunctions, just as too much dissipation can cause kidney and lung problems. Some celibates tend to redirect their pent-up sexual desire into an obsession with their religion and beliefs, or on food and diets, for example. On the other hand, plunging headfirst into sexual practices without guidance, discipline, and moderation can lead to excessive indulgence in recreational sex, or obsessions with love and/or lust. Both courses of conduct, therefore, require the instructions of an accomplished teacher to ensure that extremes do not prevent the individual from gaining the immortality that is the ultimate destination.

Some Daoists, like the famous fourth-century alchemist master Ge Hong (葛洪), believed that sexual relationships were necessary for those who sought immortality. Ge Hong stated that the sexual arts in conjunction with internal alchemy were integral if the Elixir of Immortality[6] was to be properly formed. In *The Master of Embracing Simplicity* (抱朴子, *Bao Pu Zi*), Ge Hong wrote,

> To achieve longevity and immortality, the essentials must be mastered. First, the Jing [sexual energy] must be treasured, the Qi [breath and vital energy] must be circulated, and then the great medicine must be consummated [through the infusion of the Spirit (Shen)].

To clarify the meaning of this statement further, the Jing (regenerative energy) must be made vital enough to ensure its ascent into the brain to create a powerful Spiritual Force (瑤靈, Yao Ling)[7] so the great medicine (Elixir of Immortality) can be produced and absorbed within the body. While Ge Hong believed in the importance of using sexual teachings in this process, he also acknowledged,

> It is folly to think that immortality can be attained by just sexual teachings alone. They are but a necessary and helpful adjunct to internal alchemy.

He also warned that,
> Engaging in the sexual arts incorrectly and purely on their own can be harmful and dangerous.

The Great Immortal Zhang Sanfeng shared Ge Hong's belief that the sexual teachings are a necessary component of internal alchemy. In his work *Essays on the Essentials of the Great Dao,* he explained that to attain immortality, one must study and practice the three following entrances: *Awakening the Spiritual Nature* (philosophy), *Nourishing-Life* (all the health and longevity methods, including internal alchemy), and *Harmonizing the Yin and Yang* (Daoist sexual arts).

Rather than promote one teaching over the other, however, it is best for each individual to discover the path on which he or she should focus. To illustrate this viewpoint, *The Classic on Transforming Barbarians* (化胡經, *Hua Hu Jing*) states:

> A good teacher should follow the law of appropriate response to endowments [attributes]. The most effective way is to first consider the student's nature and then respond in kind with their endowments.
>
> For some, celibacy and meditation will be most appropriate, and for others the proper guidance of the sexual teachings [Daoist sexual arts] will produce the greatest benefit.

Introduction

A well-discerning teacher will determine the proper balance of teachings and practices according to the individual.

Daoist sexual arts are considered provisional teachings; meaning, they are just a vehicle for transporting a practicer to a desired result or experience, whereupon the teachings can then be discarded. Yet, knowledge of them can truly provide great insight for all students of the Way, whether they're celibate or not. Even if for no other reason than to simply restore their regenerative energy to the state it was in when they were at their prime—a state of optimal health and vitality. Once this state is regained it provides the energy to cross over into the transformation teachings and experiences of Shen Ming (Spirit Illumination) and Yao Ling (Spiritual Force). Once these experiences are achieved, the practices are no longer needed. As the saying goes, "Why carry the boat with you once you've reached the other shore?"

Given the power of sexual/regenerative energy to propel a person forward in the process of internal alchemy, it also has the equal ability to distract one from cultivating. Most of us have been taught to link sexual activity with romance and love, or lust and pleasure. Therefore, it is essential for anyone who undertakes the Daoist sexual practices to study these teachings and shed thoughts that they are about romance, love, lust, and pleasure. When Daoist sexual practices are studied and applied correctly, with focus being on restoration and transformation, a person is then able to use the strongest of all mortal energies to leap into immortalization of the spirit.

The Internal Alchemy Connection

Internal alchemy teachings can be classified into three main areas of practice: contemplative, ritual, and dual cultivation. While contemplative internal alchemy is a matter of self-cultivation, and ceremonial and ritual practices, for the most part, rely on group participation, dual cultivation involves practice between partners, and as we find in the *Jade Tablet Decree on Nature and Life,* it can also mean an adept using self-stimulation. In this context, it is still called "dual cultivation" because both the contemplative and sexual are being employed. Knowledgeable internal alchemists will engage in all three methods of practice—at varying times and degrees—to ensure progress and completion of attaining immortality. Although this book is about sexual internal alchemy, much of the information can be applied to the contemplative practices of internal alchemy as well.

This book features translations of two important Daoist texts on the sexual practice: *The Immortaless He Xiangu on the Correct Course for Female Practice* and *The Immortal Zhang Sanfeng's Summary on Gathering the True Root-Power.* As stated previously, these texts provide a great deal of information on Daoist internal alchemy, but the terminology can be confusing, especially when key terms, such as those for Jing and Qi, are expressed in several different ways:

Terms for Jing	*Terms for Qi*
Jing (精, Essence)	Qi (氣, Vitality)
Water (水, Shui)	Fire (火, Hou)
Lead (鉛, Qian)	Mercury (汞, Gong)
White Tiger (白虎, Bai Hu)	Green Dragon (青龍, Qing Long)
Kan (坎, ☵, Water)	Li (離, ☲, Fire)
Yin (陰)	Yang (陽)

Introduction

This list would be much longer if including other Daoist works. Understand that when reading this work, however, the main focus of Daoist sexual practices is for the accumulation and preservation of sexual energy (Jing) and vital-breath energy (Qi). If you keep this purpose in mind when studying the texts, the ideas will not be difficult to grasp.

Conclusion

It's important for both female and male readers to read both texts in this book to be well informed on the purposes and different aspects of the entire practice. This helps couples identify with each other when engaging in any of the practices. When studying any work on dual cultivation, each person must understand the roles and practices of one's partner, so this book provides a balanced view of Daoist sexual practices for couples.

Another reason for understanding both texts is that the majority of bedchamber works in Chinese are Confucian in content, and written to primarily benefits males, whereas the two texts in this book are distinctly Daoist, and in Daoism the roles of males and females are equally important. Therefore, understanding and identifying with one's partner is extremely important.

Daoists view immortality in both the physical and spiritual sense, but mainly in the context of immortalizing the spirit, not the body, and with no emphasis on biological immortality. To the Daoist, sexual alchemy is not only a means of attaining immortality, but a very powerful tool for undergoing physical restoration leading to health and longevity. Unlike their Confucian counterparts, Daoist dual-cultivation practices seek to benefit everyone involved.

If undertaking these practices, be patient and progress slowly. Do not attempt to try all the procedures at once. Ideally, people will work gradually, possibly practicing once per week over a one hundred-day period. Doing so will ensure both partners learn the specifics of the methods well.

Within Zhang Sanfeng's text, there are mentions of spoken transmissions being needed to complete and realize the methods. This is true, but acquiring the instructions of a teacher is only necessary when a student has begun to sense and experience the effects of feeling the Ni Wan (fontanel area)[8] opening, or the saliva flow of the Jade Pool,[9] states in which the internal functions (movement of a fluid-like substance flowing within the body), or experiencing an illumination effect within the brain. It is important and crucial at this point to receive proper instruction before attempting to go further.

Lastly, it cannot be emphasized enough that the Daoist sexual arts are not about romance, pleasure seeking, or anything deemed as recreational sex. Those who approach these methods with thoughts of romance, pleasure, or recreation accomplish nothing because the mindset is still trapped in emotional desire of pure self-satisfaction, which is merely a form of either the desire for love and/or lust, and these are not the bases for spiritual cultivation. The biggest task for those learning these sexual practices is to approach them completely from the perspective and motivation for achieving physical restoration and spiritual transformation.

This is not to say that the emotions of romance, love, lust, and pleasure are completely void in these practices. It is really a matter of disciplining oneself not to be attached or distracted by them. One should focus on the sensations in a practice, not on

Introduction

personal fantasies or emotional bonds and needs. For these sexual practices to be effective, people need to focus completely on the sensations acquired from the stimulation, being ever mindful and attentive to what is being felt and experienced.

We raise our consciousness by feeling, listening, and responding to internal stimuli. The idea being pointed out here would be similar to that of placing a raisin in your mouth and then just chewing it a few times and swallowing. In this example, you can say you ate a raisin. On the other hand, if you were to place the raisin in your mouth, not chewing it or swallowing it, but letting the raisin dissolve in your mouth, this would be an entirely different experience. In this case, you are truly experiencing the raisin, feeling everything about the raisin on your tongue. You are sensing it, and are thus able to completely identify with the raisin. In many ways, this example of two ways for eating a raisin illustrates the difference between having sex in the recreational context and engaging in sex for restoration and spiritual purposes.

Also, keep in mind that the contents of this book are for the most part about developing a practice, and partners can choose the time and frequency of these practices. There's no implication that anyone must forego romance, pleasure, or recreation concerning sex, rather that such pursuits have their time and place in our lives. Just as we choose times and frequency for sitting in meditation, and times we do not. Sexual practices, then, are just that, a practice, and no one should apply them constantly or make them one's only expression of sexuality. Be balanced in your approach to sexual activity and practice, not fanatical.

Lastly, I wish to point out that sexual energy is a very powerful force within us—actually, the strongest force—so progress slowly. In the *Zhuang Zi* (莊周) there is a wonderful anecdotal story about taking this approach. A prince once needed to get to another vicinity quickly to deal with an emergency. After entering his carriage, the driver whipped the horses so they could leave as quickly as possible. The prince stuck his head out the window and called to his driver, "Slow up, slow up. We're in a hurry!" The prince understood that when people try to go too fast, they are likely to break down or have some accident and never get to where they are going. This is also true for people who engage in the sexual arts and practices.

---

1   *Jing*, *Qi*, and *Shen* are the Three Treasures (三寶, San Bao) of Daoist Nourishing-Life (養生) regimes and Internal Alchemy (內丹, Nei Dan) practices. *Jing* (精, essence) generally means the physical body of a human being. More specifically, the term is used in the context of bodily fluids—namely, saliva, blood, marrow, and sexual secretions. *Qi* (氣, vital-life) energy is the energy of the body that both heats and animates it, and is also the breath. *Shen* (神, spirit) is what gives the human body its mental functions and consciousness. Briefly stated, the object of Daoist Internal Alchemy is to cultivate the "Acquired" (After Heaven) aspects of these Three Treasures to restore and join the conditions of the "Innate" (Before Heaven) aspects.

Introduction

2 *Spirit Illumination* (神明, Shen Ming) is the experience of obtaining absolute clarity of the mind, wherein the intuition becomes extremely powerful and active. It's often preceded by internal visions of intense whiteness, a flashing bright light like when two streams of lightning come together. Daoists also describe it as seeing bright lights such as lanterns or stars inside the mind. For the most part, Shen Ming means reaching a state of absolute mental clarity, wherein the mind is perceived as very bright.

3 See *The Immortal: True Accounts of the 250-Year-Old Man, Li Qingyun* by Yang Sen, translated by Stuart Alve Olson (Valley Spirit Arts, 2014).

4 *Green dragon* represents "males" and "Yang energy," while *white tiger* symbolizes "females" and "Yin energy." The *path of the green dragon and white tiger,* then, signifies sexual practices.

5 All bracketed text appearing in quotes and translations are my notes and comments.

6 *Elixir of Immortality* (仙丹, Xian Dan) refers to the effects and sensations that occur when the Jing and Qi are restored to their original condition of when we were still in our mother's womb (Before Heaven or prenatal state) and then joining this with the Spirit (the Spiritual Illumination). The elixir is not a substance, rather a sensation, or perception, of transforming from mortality to immortality.

7   In Daoist internal alchemy texts this is called *Reverting Jing to the Brain* (還精補腦, Huan Jing Bu Nao). In brief, this is the process of the Jing (sexual energy) and the Qi (breath) traveling up the spine through the Du Mai meridian into the top of the head. In various other schools this process is referred to as the Stream of Life (川命, Chuan Ming) The illustration shown here is from the *Jade Tablet Decree on Nature and Life*.

8   The *Ni Wan* (泥丸, Muddy Pellet) area is where the original soft spot is situated on top of an infant's head. As Daoism explains, the skull hardens so to trap the spirit within the body. The Ni Wan is also the Qi center where one internally sees the effects of Shen Ming (Spirit Illumination).

9   See the section on the *Jade Pool Effect* in the Appendix.

Book One

女功正法何仙姑著

Nu Gong Zheng Fa He Xian Gu Zhe

The Immortaless He Xiangu on the Correct Course for Female Practice

A Discourse and Illustration on the Female Practices of Refining the Self and Reverting the Elixir

女功煉己還丹圖說
Nu Gong Lian Ji Huan Dan Tu Shuo

[Text on forehead] 顖門, Xin Men (fontanel on top of the head). [Cheeks] 準頭, Zhun Tou (tip of the nose). [Chin] 玄膺, Xuan Ying (mouth, the Mysterious Receiver). [Throat] 十二重樓, Shi Er Zhong Lou (esophagus, Twelve-Storied Pagoda). [Breasts] 乳房穴, Ru Fang Xue (Breast Chamber Points). [Stomach] 絳宮, Jiang Gong (solar plexus, the Bright Red Palace). [Center of abdomen] 中極, Zhong Ji (Center of the Ultimate, Dan Tian). [Between the legs] 血海, Xue Hai (Sea of Blood, the vagina).

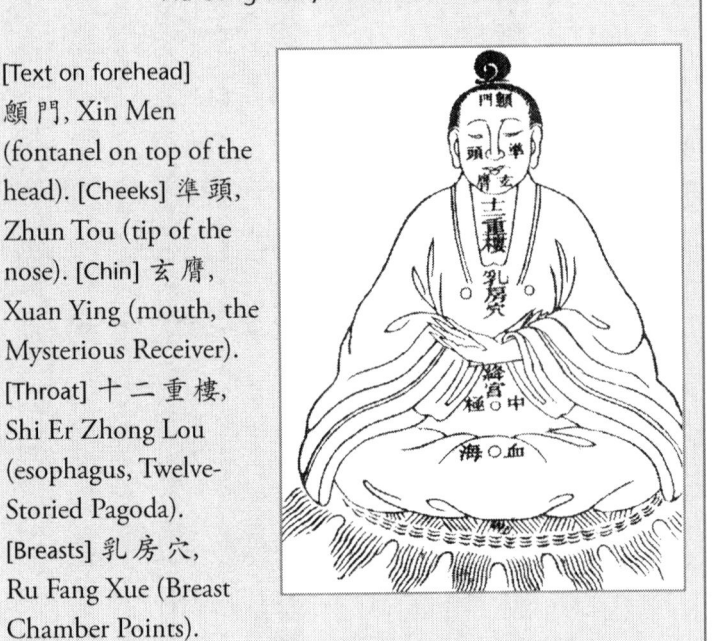

From *The Illustrated Book of Female Practices of Refining the Self and Reverting the Elixir* (early Qing dynasty). Reproduced in the 1906 edition of *A Treatise on the Uniting of the Female Elixir* (女彈合編, Nu Dan He Bian).

He Xiangu's Introduction

At the age of sixteen a male's sexual energy [Jing] becomes fully functional, and when the sexual energy becomes full, the male begins to dissipate it. At age fourteen, a female's menses begins to appear and when the menses begins to fully flow each month, it overflows [and so dissipates]. If males seek to avoid dissipating and females wish to avoid overflowing,[1] they must come to understand *Wind* and *Fire*. Fire is the "Original Spirit," and Wind is the "True Breath." Bringing the spirit and breath into harmonious balance is accomplished by gaining inner mindfulness. The method is to direct the gaze from the Mysterious Pass[2] in the two eyes to the Qi point between them. The concentration of the breath [Qi] and spirit [Shen] is rooted in the function of mental absorption. When the natural Wind and Fire continually interact, this transforms the Jing and augments the Qi, transforms the Qi and augments the Shen. When the Shen has been perfected and the body transformed, then there is a body beyond the body.

An aphorism says:

If constantly keeping and focusing the spirit and breath, the body will be transformed and the Jade Secretion[3] will flow. Relying entirely on the Cavern of Immortality, the Yang Spirit is then refined and will manifest at the Supreme Gate.[4]

Understand that all living creatures will certainly die, but we must also understand that when Original Spirit[5] dies, it can undergo rebirth.

If getting the spirit of the mind[6] to dwell within the Qi, the embryo[7] will then be properly nourished and the attainment of immortality is assured.

In practicing this way, what possible danger is there of the internal elixir failing?

The purpose of these methods is to open the Ren Mai and Du Mai subtle meridians.[8] The circulation is internal and external of the Central Pass, and it is here where the female's practice is a little different. The activity begins in the breasts, or Upper Pass, continues down to the navel, or Central Pass, and then ends by returning to the womb, or Lower Pass. Later, the Middle and Lower are transformed into just one point.[9] When a male refines his Jing, this is called Ultimate Yang Qi [太陽氣, Tai Yang Qi]. When a female refines her menses this is called Ultimate Yin Qi [太陰氣, Tai Yin Qi].

The secret of Fire and Wind is in knowing the appropriate use of the Before Heaven and After Heaven [breathing].

The Before Heaven is employed in the middle and the After Heaven at the beginning and end.[10]

While practicing Lesser Heavenly circulation, do not forget both "contemplation" and "tranquility" during the Four Intervals[11] of the twelve [Chinese] hours. Whatever the mind imagines can be accomplished, and those who can hold onto and join the Before Heaven Qi and the After Heaven Qi will feel as if intoxicated [euphoric] the entire day.

Ordinary females of the world are too deeply attached to convention. They also ingest too many fleshy foods and are easily given to erroneous romantic thoughts. When they become attracted to a man, ideas of marriage delude them, but

Book One: The Correct Course for Female Practice

Image of the Body Refining the Jade Essences

[First panel of text, right side]
Within, there exists a distinct Heaven in a minuscule gourd. The Iron Ox plows the earth to plant the golden lotus. This is like the treasures of a home. When the home is established, who then does not study immortality?

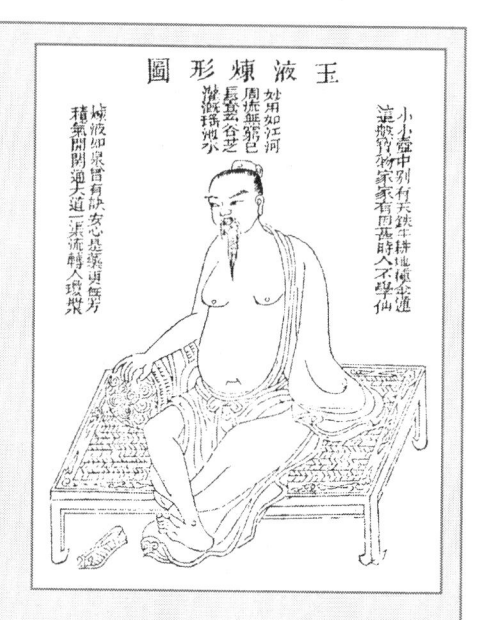

[Middle panel of text]
Like rivers and streams the uses are so profound. Circulating and flowing without limit or cessation. Constantly nourishing the herb of longevity in the Mysterious Valley, and irrigating the water of the Jade Pool.

[Third panel of text, left side]
Refining the secretions is like the gathering of fountain springs. There is a secret for a calm mind, and it is to have endless joy. Accumulate the Qi, open the passes, and penetrate the Great Dao. A person's nectar flows and turns about the one wheel.

From the *Jade Tablet Decree on Nature and Life*

then they become regretful in their hearts. In the spring they are motivated by love, but in the autumn they feel harmed, sometimes to the point of suffering from consumption. From indulging in raw and cold foods their menses becomes irregular. Additionally, they are easily led astray by their emotions so that both their bodies and natural attributes are destroyed. They then spend all their days affected by dissatisfaction.

Everyone should take a lesson from this and not create negative retributions. Those who persevere know peace within themselves; those who repent know happiness. The mind is content and the heart is like still water. In meditation one should constantly emulate the Golden Statues with the mouth closed and tongue concealed. In movement or stillness, in words and deeds, be dedicated and yet humble. Break down the barrier of emotions and leap out from the sea of negative desires.

> **Nature and Life**
>
> 性 命
>
> Xing Ming
>
> *Cultivating Life is Wei* [為, Doing];
> *Cultivating Nature is Wu Wei* [無為, Non-Doing].
> *First cultivate Life and naturally Nature will arrive.*

The time of puberty in the human body is the wellspring for the cultivation of Life [Ming].[12] By seeking the proper training methods soon, this period [of puberty] may be transformed through refinement into Essence [Nature, Xing]. When practices are performed over a long time, the spirit

Book One: The Correct Course for Female Practice

returns to Heaven above. You seekers of the Way [道, Dao] should motivate yourselves.

First, all females must pay attention to curing the problems of the menstrual flow. Before pregnancy or following childbirth there may be blockage of the menses causing illness. In such cases, include daily waist massage to your practice, thirty-six times to the left and right. Do the same for the shoulders, moving them up and down and to the left and right each thirty-six times. Lastly, massage the center of the navel with the two hands interlaced, rubbing seventy-two times in each direction. When the body feels warm internally, stop.

If profuse bleeding occurs during menses or vaginal discharge, then proceed to the exercise of Hanging Tiger [吊虎, Diao Hu]. This simply means hanging yourself upside down by your feet from a horizontal beam. The body takes on the appearance of a golden hook, with the palms resting on the ground for support. Mentally focus on the area below the navel and make a complete orbit of Qi by imagining it circling to the left and right each 120 times.

If the female needs to cure blocked menses, stagnant blood, or swelling in the lower abdomen, she should perform Hanging Sea Tortoise [吊海龜, Diao Hai Gui], but doing so right side up. Hang [by the hands] from a horizontal beam with the palms together and the toes touching the ground. With eyes closed and head lowered, contemplate the heart [solar plexus] with thirty-six breaths. Then the mind should focus one inch behind the navel for thirty-six breaths. The eyes then contemplate the afflicted area [vagina] with thirty-six breaths. This will eliminate every kind of affliction. Employing the secret of using the heated Qi [breath], directed by the mind-intent, will cure illness. This secret method of curing illness was first handed down from the immortaless attendants of Xi Wangmu.

---

1. Males damage their vitality and Jing from dissipating their semen. Females damage their vitality and Jing through their menstrual flow, so they need to engage in practices to lessen their menses. Practices such as the Tiger's Waist Exercise (sometimes called Swimming Dragon or Triple Bracelets Encircling the Moon), the Doe Exercises (sometimes called Healing Tigress Exercises), foregoing eating raw and cold foods, Hanging Tiger and Hanging Sea Tortoise practices, using the Jade Stem, stimulating orgasm more frequently, and ingesting certain herbs, especially Dong Quai, all help reduce the menstrual flow. See Appendix for more information on these practices.

2. *Mysterious Pass* (玄關, Xuan Guan) refers to the area of the Third Eye. *Qi points* (氣穴, Qi Xue) are focal points of concentrated Qi along a meridian (in this case, the Ren Mai).

Book One: The Correct Course for Female Practice

3   *Jade Secretion* (玉液, Yu Yi) is a reference to the saliva, which along with the sexual secretions, bone marrow, tears, and blood are considered the *True Water* or *Lead* in internal alchemy; but, more so, the term "Jade Secretion" is referring to the *Three Great Medicines* or *Three Peak Medicines* (甘露, Gan Lu)—also known as Amrita or Sweet Dew. These medicines, or elixirs, are produced when heightened ecstatic states of sexual stimulation are achieved. The first is the Upper Peak Medicine, exuding from two cavities under the tongue along each side of the frenulum. The Upper Peak Medicine is also called Red Lotus Peak Elixir and is grayish with a hint of red in color. The Middle Peak Medicine, or Double Lotus Peak Elixir, is whitish with a hint of yellow in color and is produced in a cavity directly below each breast nipple. The Lower Peak Medicine, or Purple Mushroom Elixir, is clear with a hint of purple in color, and comes forth from a cavity directly beneath the clitoris. In males, the Lower Peak Medicine is contained within the clear pre-ejaculatory fluid.

4   *Cavern of Immortality* (仙洞, Xian Dong) is another name for the Hui Yin (perineum Qi center). *Yang Spirit* (陽神, Yang Shen) is the refined energies of Jing and Qi moving in the body. *Supreme Gate* (太門, Tai Men) is another term for the Mysterious Pass or Third Eye.

5   *Original Spirit* (元神, Yuan Shen) is the Before Heaven (prenatal) spirit that enters into our mother's womb at conception. The Original Spirit is different from what we normally think of as just "spirit," or as mentioned in this text, the "Spirit of the Mind," which is the After Heaven (postnatal) condition. The Original Spirit is also called the Before Heaven Spirit, True Spirit, the "innate" or "primordial" spirit. To understand the difference here we only need consider that before the umbilical cord is severed, we exist in the Before Heaven condition (i.e., with True Jing, True Qi, and True Spirit). The After Heaven, then, is referring to the Essence, Vitality, and Spirit that is "acquired," from our practices and habits. Internal alchemy then uses the After Heaven to help us revert to the Before Heaven, or, in other terms, we use the acquired Qi (through practice) to restore the innate Qi.

6   *Spirit of the mind* (心神, Xin Shen). This is the conscious mind.

7   *Embryo* (胎, Tai) refers to the idea of creating a spiritual fetus within the abdomen—lower Dan Tian (Elixir Field).

8   *Ren Mai* (任脈, Function Vessel) and *Du Mai* (督脈, Control Vessel) are the two main Qi meridians that run along the front (Ren Mai) and back (Du Mai) of the body. Illustration from *Tai Ji Qi: Fundamentals of Qigong, Meditation, and Internal Alchemy*, vol. 1 Chen Kung Series (Valley Spirit Arts, 2013).

Book One: The Correct Course for Female Practice

9   The *Three Passes* on the front of the body, sometimes translated as *Barriers*, are normally referred to as the Upper, Middle, and Lower Dan Tians (Elixir Fields).

In the illustration to the right, which is specific to females, the Upper Pass (上關, Shang Guan) is the Bright Palace (solar plexus). The Middle Pass (中關, Zhong Guan) is behind the navel (Dan Tian of the abdomen), and the Lower Pass (下關, Xia Guan) is the womb.

Note that for females, the Three Passes on the front of the body are different from those of males, but the ones on the back are the same. See also the illustration and text on p. 52.

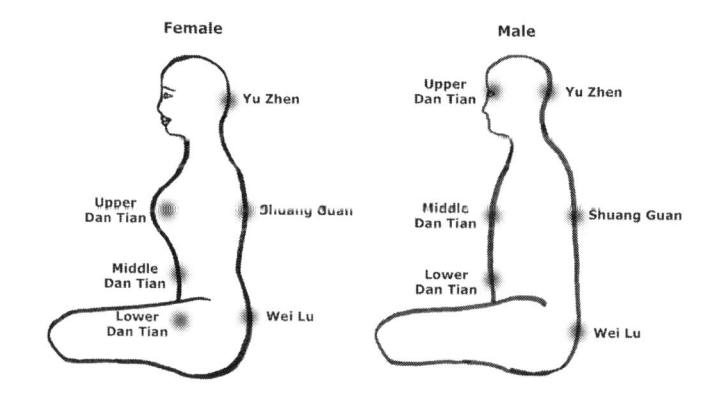

10 *Before Heaven* (embryonic breathing) and *After Heaven* (natural breathing) are important fundamentals of internal alchemy. *Embryonic Breathing* (胎息, Tai Xi) is normally referred to as "reverse breathing." In "natural breathing," the abdomen is expanded when inhaling, and contracted when exhaling. Embryonic Breathing is the opposite. The abdomen contracts during inhalation and expands during exhalation, which is why it's sometimes called "Reverse Breathing." In Embryonic Breathing, the inhalation provides a greater force and energy for pushing Qi up the back of the spine, and, with the exhalation, driving Qi down the front of the body. It is called "Embryonic Breathing" because this is how we breathed when still within our mother's womb, and so this type of breathing recalls this state and enhances the idea of creating a Spirit Embryo. Daoist cultivators should use After Heaven breathing until the Jing, Qi, and Shen have been replenished, a condition of fullness as it was in our youth when still experiencing the effects of our Before Heaven endowments (the True Jing, Qi, and Shen), then switch to Before Heaven breathing to move the elixir. Once the *Nine Revolutions of the Elixir* has been accomplished, cultivators should return to After Heaven breathing.

Book One: The Correct Course for Female Practice

11 *The Four Intervals* is a reference to the four periods of the day when it is most auspicious to practice. In some Daoist texts these are referred to as "firing times," meaning the correct times to heat the cauldron. The Four Intervals include the hour of Zi (子, 11:00 p.m. to 1:00 a.m.); the hour of Mao (卯, 5:00 a.m. to 7:00 a.m.); the hour of Wu (午, 11:00 a.m. to 1:00 p.m.); and the hour of You (酉, 5:00 p.m. to 7:00 p.m.).

12 *Nature* and *Life* (性命, Xing Ming): These two terms are the main headings of all self-cultivation in Daoism. Life (Ming) is considered the "doing" practices, such as Nourishing-Life Arts, sexual alchemy, and so forth. Nature (Xing) is the state of "non-doing" and entering the Void, more succinctly the state of tranquility.

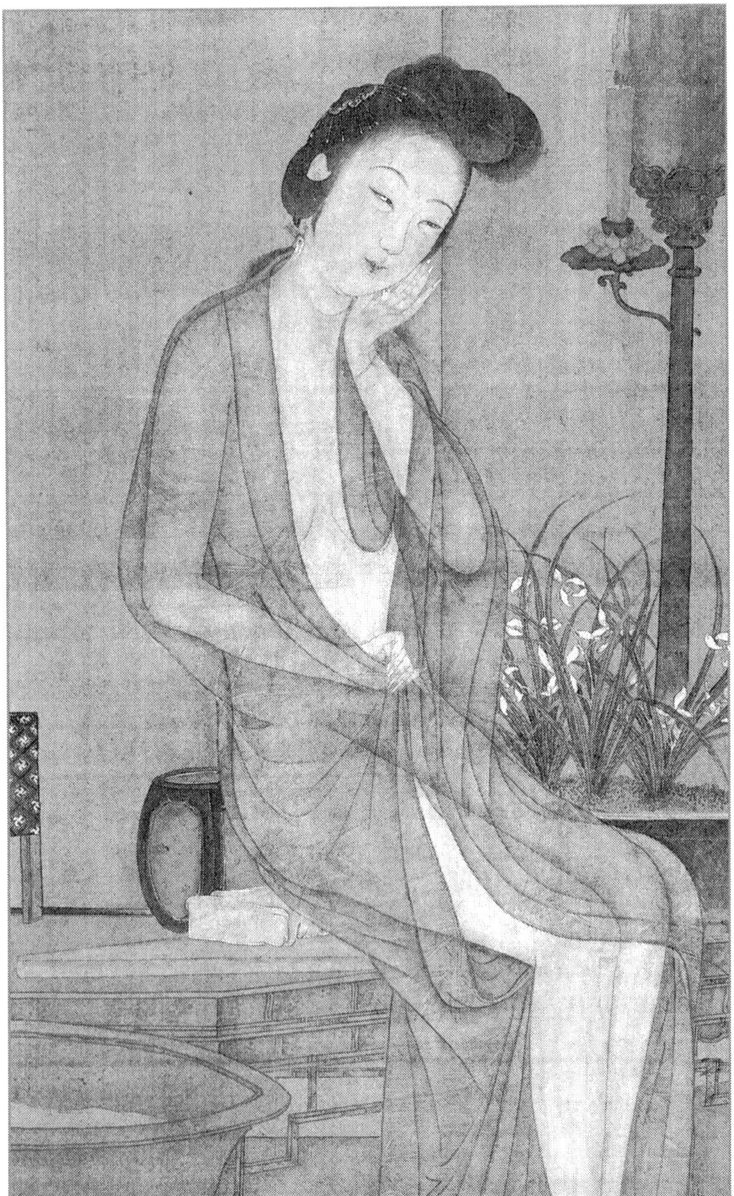

Chapter One

Laying the Foundation and Purifying the Heart

築 基 净 心

Zhu Ji Jing Xin

In seeking to set up the foundation, the heart must be purified first. When not a speck of dust remains to pollute us, we will never go astray in the world. When the heart is empty and desires are purified, there naturally is a sense of Tranquility [靜, Jing], and with the Clarity [清, Qing] of a mirror or the transparency of water, the heart is now pure. We may now speak of setting up the foundation.

Females belong by nature to the Kun[1] principle. Her back is Yin and her front Yang. The breasts are the external orifices, and the Breast Streams [cavities under the nipples] are the internal points. In sitting, first *Ride the Crane*,[2] with legs and knees placed one upon the other. Tightly lock the Lower Pass[3] to secure the Before Heaven Qi. Move the breath to the Upper Pass[4] and avoid leakage from the Lower Pass. The Middle Pass is 1.3 fen [0.17 inches] behind the navel.

> ## Clarity and Tranquility
> 清 靜
> Qing Jing
> *Clarity purifies the Heart, and Tranquility purifies the Spirit.*
> *When the Heart moves the Spirit, then immortality can be attained.*

If wishing to avoid the Five Leaks [Five Senses], the Three Passes must be guarded. The senses of hearing and sight should be constantly directed within, and the mouth closed without speech. The Qi should be concentrated in the Breast Streams and the Spirit focused in the Golden Chamber [between the eyes]. Revert to the One and concentrate the mind. The Golden Mother[5] is focused in the heart, Lao Zi [老子] in the nasal orifice, and the Buddha [佛, Fo] on the tip of the nose. The tail of the nose is called the Base of the Mountain [山根, Shan Gen] and is located between the two eyes. The sages have considered this the point at which to practice stillness. If one can faithfully maintain this, it is the focal point of the highest good.

When sixteen, recollect the time before the onset [puberty] of the Seven Emotions,[6] which are absent and the Five Attributes[7] which are empty. The heart is always content, and one is sprightly and full of life, like my teacher, Master Lu [Dongbin]. When the Source of Dao is jade pure, concentrate the spirit at the lower Dan Tian [womb]. Consciousness issues from between the eyes and is drawn down to the Dan Tian. The Before Heaven Qi arrives, and the After Heaven Qi enters. Painstakingly preserve them.

Book One: The Correct Course for Female Practice

The female's Breast Stream is her Upper Elixir Point. The location behind the navel and in front of the kidneys is the Middle Pass. The Female Gate is the Lower Pass. The womb is the crucible. Now draw the consciousness down from between the eyes to the Breast Stream and then to the navel and the womb, creating a single connecting pathway. The Primordial Seeds are the source of life. A male's Original Jing[8] is the highest Yang Qi. The female's blood is the highest Yin Qi. These are the treasures that give life to the body and are the root of the myriad transformations. The male stores it in the Qi cavity of the Gate of Life [命門, Ming Men, the kidneys]. The female stores it in the uterus [Feminine Gate]. When passion stirs, it is difficult to preserve them, but when the heart is still, they may be protected. However, one needs both Wind and Fire to refine and transform them so that they are forever preserved.

---

1   *Kun* (坤, *The Receptivity of Earth*) is the second image in the *Book of Changes*. It is represented by six Yin (broken) lines (☷) and symbolizes the female.

2. *Ride the Crane* (騎鶴, Qi He) is the same position one would make when riding a horse side saddle.

    The illustration shown here, titled "The Immortaless He Xiangu Ascending to Heaven Upon a Crane" is from her treatise, *The Correct Course for Female Practice*.

3. *Lower Pass* is the "Fountain Gate" (噴門, Pen Men), vaginal opening and the womb area of the female's lower body.

4. The *Upper Pass* in females equates to the solar plexus, the *Middle Pass* is the Dan Tian (behind the navel), and the *Lower Pass* is the womb and vaginal opening. See the illustration on page 37, note 9.

5. The *Golden Mother* (西王母) is Xi Wangmu, but in this case her immortal name Jin Mu (金母) is used.

6. The *Seven Emotions* or *Seven Earthly Spirits* (七魄, Qi Po): happiness, sorrow, anger, anxiety, fear, grief, and love/lust. The seventh emotion is a dual term for the reason that females are typically more affected by love, whereas males are affected by lust.

Book One: The Correct Course for Female Practice

7   The *Five Attributes* (五陰, Wu Yin): formations, feelings, perceptions, impulses, and consciousnesses.

8   *Original Jing* (元精, Yuan Jing) refers to the Before Heaven regenerative energy we had before the umbilical cord was cut.

Chapter Two

Cultivating the Menses
月事修

Yue Shi Xiu

At fourteen a female's menses begins and her blood becomes deficient. Although every month the menstrual flow is replenished, in reality, every month brings injury and waste. Postmenopausal females who desire to cultivate the menses through refinement and transformation must first cause it to return. Refrain from eating raw or cold foods to avoid stagnation of the blood. However, because the menstrual flow is the very foundation of life, the method for beginning to refine it involves deliberate action so it transforms and increases the blood and Qi so that there will be no further injury. *Existence is the beginning of nonexistence; nonexistence is the end of existence* [from the *Dao De Jing*].

Before Heaven Qi
先 天 氣
Xian Tian Qi

The Before Heaven Qi is what you were endowed with at birth from the parents.

> **After Heaven Qi**
>
> 後 天 氣
>
> Hou Tian Qi
>
> *The After Heaven Qi is what you cultivate from practices.*
> *When the two coalesce in the Elixir Field, immortality is yours.*

Where there is a specific [Qi] point, use effort so that the After Heaven Qi can flow freely; where there is no specific point, use the mind so that the Before Heaven Qi becomes full.[1] Wherever the mind goes the eye follows, and the spirit and breath [Qi] are coordinated. This process transforms the blood and increases the Qi, refines the Qi and nourishes the spirit. Begin with the Middle Pass and deliberately raise the Qi straight up thirty-six times. Raising it to the Upper Pass, cause it to revolve thirty-six times each to the left and right. Now direct it to the breasts and revolve it thirty-six times each to the left and right. The mind should direct the eye to focus on the Upper and Lower Passes. Interlace the fingers of the two hands and place them over the area below the navel and above the fountain [the womb].

Now, as if using conscious effort, raise the Qi directly up thirty-six times. Bring it up to the Breast Stream and then to the inside of the external orifices [the nipples] of the breasts. Revolve to the left and right each thirty-six times.[2]

Book One: The Correct Course for Female Practice

1 When using the *After Heaven* breath, methods for focusing on Qi points and meridians are employed. With *Before Heaven* breathing, "free circulation of breath" is used.

2 This section references the *Healing Tigress Exercises* (Doe Exercises), wherein several methods are given for restoring the breasts. The breasts are the external expression of Qi in females, and they are the location of their Upper Dan Tian. So, in the Healing Tigress Exercises, the vaginal area (Lower Dan Tian), navel region (Middle Dan Tian), and the breasts (Upper Dan Tian) are focused on with specific exercises.

Chapter Three

Slaying the Dragon

殺 龍

Sha Long

The secret method for Slaying the Dragon [reducing the menstrual flow] involves deliberate action. At the Zi and Wu hours[1] sit as if Mounted on a Crane[2] and knock the teeth together seventy-two times. Using After Heaven Qi [natural breathing], breathe through the nose naturally for a count of thirty-six, and the meridians of the whole body will open. The heel should firmly press against the Jade Gate [玉門, Yu Men, the vaginal opening]. Interlace the fingers and place them under the navel. Now deliberately raise the Qi straight up thirty-six times, by bringing the Qi to the Upper Pass [solar plexus]. Use the imagination to revolve it in each direction thirty-six times. Then follow this by extending the Qi to the Middle Pass [lower Elixir Field, Dan Tian, abdomen] and revolve it with the imagination in each direction thirty-six times. The hands are then raised up as if pressing up against Heaven in a relaxed manner thirty-six times and then in a more quick and urgent manner thirty-six times.

When there is a sudden movement in the Wei Lu [尾閭, Tail Gateway, the tailbone area], place the two hands on the sides of the waist, grind the teeth tightly and raise the shoulders straight up. When the Double Pass feels activated, deliberately straighten the head and back, raise the Qi to the Jade Pillow [occiput] and then all the way to the Muddy Pellet [Ni Wan, top of

Three Barriers/Passes
Three on the Back (Same for Males and Females)

三 關

San Guan

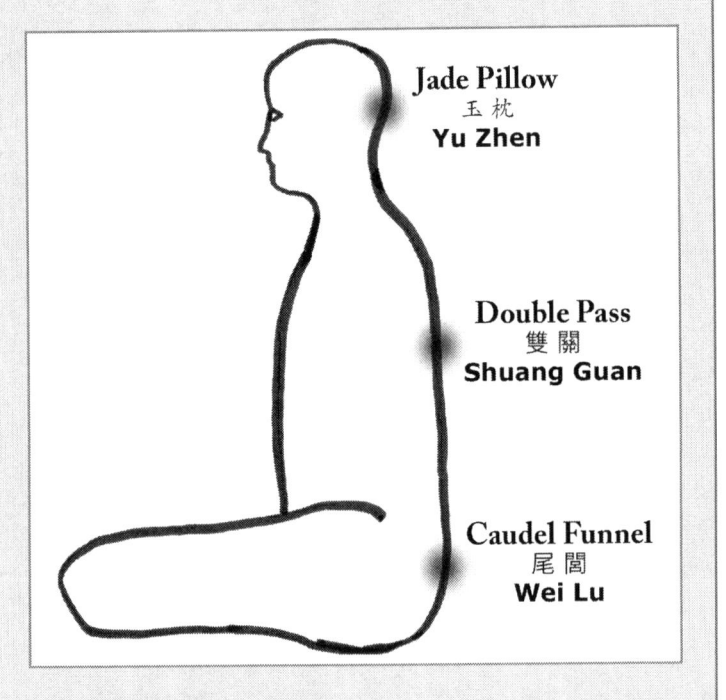

Jade Pillow
玉枕
Yu Zhen

Double Pass
雙關
Shuang Guan

Caudel Funnel
尾閭
Wei Lu

Reversing the flow of the elixir is to first transport it to the Wei Lu, then up to the Double Pass, and then the Jade Pillow.

Once in the Jade Pillow, the Mind-Intent will carry the Elixir into the Muddy Pellet.

Book One: The Correct Course for Female Practice

the head]. Once this is complete, press the lower lip tightly against the upper lip, and using the Mind-Intent [意, Yi, the imagination], send the True Qi [真氣, Zhen Qi] up to the Muddy Pellet and down through the nasal orifice.

When the tongue touches the Heavenly Bridge [天橋, Tian Qiao, top of the palate], the Sweet Dew [甘露, Gan Lu] flows naturally. With one contraction of the nose, the saliva is deliberately swallowed and directed down to the area below the navel. Place the hand on the female part [the Jade Gate, vagina], and gently press inward towards the womb thirty-six times. When the Sweet Dew enters the crucible, the warmed Qi begins to circulate. The heel of the foot should be pressed tightly against the Jade Gate [vagina], and body and mind should both be calm. The womb is now settled and peaceful.

It may be that a female will need to re-establish her menses after menopause.[3] Therefore, if the menstrual flow has already or is beginning to become dried, it is then necessary to begin restoring it. The method is to mentally raise the Qi as employed in the practice of Slaying the Dragon, but the process should be reversed to make the menses return. So, instead of gently rubbing left and right with the hands circularly on the surface of the skin, this should be changed to a firm pressing into the body, and circling left and right. In one hundred days the menses will return. Now wait three days and then apply the previous practices. After another hundred days the practice will be complete and the dragon will be slain.

Daoist Sexual Arts

---

1   The hour of Zi runs from 11:00 p.m. to 1:00 a.m., and the hour of Wu from 11:00 a.m. to 1:00 p.m.

2   *Mounted on a Crane* is the same as *Riding a Crane*.

3   Daoist female practice indicates, on one hand, that the menstrual flow should be reduced, but, on the other hand, to re-establish it for those who have gone through menopause. The idea is that if a female is still producing menstrual flow she should reduce it. However, if a female comes to these practices in her senior years and has gone through menopause, she needs to re-establish it so that she can then regulate it, which is the goal of how females preserve Jing.

Chapter Four

Restore the Breasts to Youthfulness

复乳青春

Fu Ru Qing Chun

The breasts are connected with the heart and lungs above and to the Ocean of Qi[1] below. If one wishes to train the breasts so that they acquire the shape of a young girl's, the method is in Slaying the Dragon. Increase and direct the Sweet Dew[2] straight to the Crimson Palace.[3] Focus the mind on the two breasts and revolve them to the left and right thirty-six times each. The lips are pressed together above and below, the teeth are clamped together tightly, and the nostrils are closed to make use of the true internal breathing.

> **Embryo Breathing**
>
> 胎 息
>
> Tai Xi
>
> *This is True Breath of the Immortals.*[40]
> *Internal Breathing is Embryo Breath.*
> *Embryo Breathing is the Before Heaven Breath.*
> *Before Heaven Breathing is In-the-Womb Breath.*
> *Do you remember?*

Place the palms of the two hands onto the breasts, massaging each in a circular fashion to the left and right seventy-two times. First use relaxed pressure and then stronger; first light pressure and then heavy pressure. In one hundred days, your training will be complete and the areolae will acquire the shape of large walnuts.[4]

In the *Secrets on Refining the Breasts* [煉乳訣, Lian Ru Jue], it is said:

> The left breast is the sun and the right breast is the moon: one Yang and one Yin.
>
> The internal circulation of the Qi through the nasal passage is called "Turning the Big Dipper."[5]
>
> If seeking Yin and Yang to revert, look to the sun and moon.[6] The True Fire must be cultivated in the two palms.[7]

Book One: The Correct Course for Female Practice

1. *Ocean of Qi* (氣海, Qi Hai) is a Qi center located three inches below the navel and one inch inward.

2. See the *Jade Pool Effect* in the Appendix for more information on cultivating Sweet Dew.

3. *Crimson Palace* (絳宮, Jiang Gong) is a Qi center in the solar plexus region.

4. The swelling and enlargement of the areolae and nipples are as crucial to females in generating Jing as it is for males to be able to produce erections. The breasts are the feminine expression of Qi. Therefore, the more blood and Qi concentrated in them the greater the Jing energy will be. In Taboo Girl and White Tigress Green Dragon schools, females were taught to use suction cups, such as those used in Moxibustion treatments, to draw large quantities of blood into the areolae and nipples until they resemble large walnuts.

5. Daoist internal alchemy suggests that the movement of Qi through the Ren Mai and Du Mai meridians is identical to the turning of the handle of the Big Dipper as it moves across the sky.

6. This line could also be translated as, "Seeking Yin and Yang to fuse as one, put your gaze between the sun and moon, the two eyes."

7   *True Fire,* meaning the Before Heaven Qi, is generated through stimulating the Dragon and Tiger cavities in the middle of the two palms. Dragon is the left palm, and Tiger the right. This is accomplished by folding the fingers into the palm and then putting some pressure with the middle finger to press into the Qi center. Then while focusing on the Third Eye, the Qi can pass through the nasal passage with greater ease.

Chapter Five

Establishing the Crucible and Creating the Fetus

成鼎生胎

Cheng Ding Sheng Tai

For males, the Lower, Middle, and Upper Dan Tians are the crucibles. For females, the womb, navel, and Breast Streams are the crucibles. The womb is 1.3 fen [0.17 inches] from the Lower Dan Tian and 2.8 fen [0.37 inches] from the navel. It is also located below the Upper Pass, or breasts. Above is the Breast Stream, in the Middle is the navel, and in the Lower is the womb. The locations extend from the external to the internal, but their function is from the internal to the external. The male is without a womb and instead takes the Dan Tian as the great crucible. Although the names are the same, what they point to is different.

Crucible and Stove

鼎炉

Ding Lu

The Crucible contains; the Stove heats. Jing is Water and Qi is Fire. Capture the vapors and condense it into the Elixir.

When the Before Heaven Qi coalesces with the After Heaven Qi in the Crucible, this is the Elixir.

Master Lu's *Secret of the Golden Flower* [金花宗旨, *Jin Hua Zong Zhi*] states, "It is the two eyes that Return the Light [回光, Hui Guang]."

From the point between the eyes, concentrate the mind and focus it on the Lower Dan Tian. After the female has completed the training methods for Slaying the Dragon, she should relax for a few moments and then Return the Light from the point between the eyes and deliberately direct it to the Breast Stream thirty-six times. Then direct it to the Lower Dan Tian thirty-six times. Use the mind to draw the water [saliva] from the Pool of Flowers [花池, Hua Chi, the mouth] to the Upper Crucible [the breasts], and drawing the secretions over to the heart and lung regions as well. With the Mind-Intent, direct the heat to the Upper Crucible. After this, deliberately direct it down to the Middle Crucible [navel], and then to the Great Crucible [the womb], where it is revolves eighteen times. When it is hot internally, the fire rises; when the crucible has been established, and the embryo is created.

Chapter Six

Self-Regulate Embryonic Breathing

自 調 胎 息

Zi Diao Tai Xi

If able to avoid breathing errors such as panting, roughness, and shallowness, then the breath generated through the nose will become well regulated. When every breath reverts to the root [lower abdomen], this then is the Embryonic Breath. As long as the breath moves, there is a pulse moving throughout the blood vessels, but if the breath is halted, the pulses stop [Bi Qi, 閉氣 to stop or close off the breath].

An ancient text states: "Just breathing in the Qi does not lead to longevity; the Qi must be captured and accumulated for longevity to be obtained." When the True Breath circulates, the Qi can be accumulated.

After practicing Slaying the Dragon, rest momentarily. When the Seven Emotions [七情, Qi Qing] and random thoughts no longer arise, press the heel of the foot up against the Jade Gate, close the lips together to conceal the teeth, and let the mind visualize on the 3.8-fen [.5 inch] distance between the heart and kidneys.[1] Revolve the Qi to the left and right for forty-nine breaths. When the Sweet Dew comes naturally, imagine swallowing and raising the Qi.[2]

> ## The Seven Emotions
>
> ## 七情
>
> Qi Qing
>
> *Happiness, Anger, Sorrow, Fear, Anxiety, Hate, Love/Lust*
>
> 喜　怒　哀　懼　憂　惡　愛 / 欲
>
> Xi　Nu　Ai　Ju　You　E　Ai/Yu
>
> *These Seven Emotions are the energies from which the Seven Earthly Spirits are nourished.*
>
> ## The Seven Earthly Spirits
>
> ## 七魄
>
> Qi Po
>
> *Regulate the emotions and the Earthly Spirits are subdued.*

Raising means to cause it to revert to the navel. The Qi then becomes concentrated and after a long time turns into the Embryonic Breath. By not attempting to exhale, the exhalation comes naturally; by not attempting to inhale, the inhalation comes naturally; and by not attempting to raise anything, the ascent comes naturally. Within the Jade Gate is a natural opening and closing. Naturally and gently, the elixir comes into being of itself.

Book One: The Correct Course for Female Practice

1. This is the juncture where the Ren Mai meets with the Dai Mai (帶脈, Belt Meridian).

2. Within the description of the *Seven Emotions,* the emotions of "love" and "lust" are placed together. Daoists claim that *love* is the emotion that most adversely affects women, while *lust* most adversely affects men. In other lists of these Seven Emotions, "anxiety" replaces love, and lust is the final seventh one. The translation/usage presented here is also found in the work of Li Qingyun and it appears to be more accurate in the sense of there being seven distinct emotions, as *anxiety* is definitely an emotion.

Chapter Seven

Return the Fluid to Form the Fetus
復 液 因 胎
Fu Ye Yin Tai

With the male practice of the River Cart [河車, He Che], the spirit is Fire and the breath is Wind. The male daily gathers these and returns them to the stove, where they are refined into the Lesser Medicine, so when the Qi has been accumulated in abundance the spirit is perfected and the Greater Medicine[1] forms. When the Five Dragons [五龍, Wu Long] serve the sage and the circulation becomes natural, then move from the Lower Dan Tian to the Middle Dan Tian. As the Qi increases and the spirit is nourished, shift the attention to the Upper Dan Tian. First penetrate the Highest Gate [Muddy Pellet] and the Jade Liquid will revert to become the elixir, just like clarified butter[2] saturating the crown of the head. When the Yang Spirit has been completely balanced, this then is called becoming an immortal.

> ## Lesser Medicine, Greater Medicine
> 小 藥 大 藥
> Xiao Yao Da Yao
>
> *The Lesser Medicine is produced by the practices of the After Heaven methods of replenishing the Three Treasures. The Greater Medicine is produced from the Before Heaven method of Returning the Spirit to Emptiness.*

If asking, "What is the female's *Jade Liquid reverting to become the elixir,*" it is the Red Dragon being transformed into the White Phoenix.[3] When it fills the Lower Field, it is like gestating a fetus. After one's practice is complete, the Qi is transformed and the spirit becomes like a luminous perfect sphere. As it passes through the Highest Gate it approaches the state of Yang Spirit. Never departing from the above practice, it is as though emulating the Immortaless Guan Yin atop Mount Potala.[4]

Book One: The Correct Course for Female Practice

1 The *Lesser Medicine* is what we acquire in the After Heaven, postnatal, sense of cultivation. The *Greater Medicine* comes from the restoration of the Before Heaven, prenatal, condition.

2 See p. 78 of *The Immortal: True Accounts of the 250-Year-Old Man, Li Qingyun* by Yang Sen (Valley Spirit Arts, 2014) for a fuller explanation of this effect and practice.

3 The *Red Dragon* (紅龍, Hong Long) is referring to the tongue and the *White Phoenix* (白鳳, Bai Feng) is the transformed saliva (Jade Secretion). As one cultivates and refines the Jade Secretion, the saliva will turn very white and thick in consistency —emulating male semen in appearance. This refined fluid then gathers in the lower Dan Tian to form the spiritual fetus. Much like sperm attaching to the egg. See *Jade Pool Effect* in the Appendix.

4 The text is saying that in producing the Amrita, Sweet Dew, or Divine Nectar, it is like the stories of Guan Yin pouring the nectar from her vase to enlighten or immortalize deserving cultivators.

Chapter Eight

Refining and Transforming the Yang Spirit

煉化陽神

Lian Hua Yang Shen

The first task for males is to transform the Jing [sexual secretions] so to increase the Qi, then the Qi must be refined into Spirit [Shen], and this is how males create the internal elixir. The initial task for a female is to first transform the blood to increase the Qi, then refine the Qi into Spirit, and this is how a female creates the internal elixir. Both use Fire and Wind. As for the female Slaying the Dragon, this consists of transforming the blood into Qi. It also is said she must regulate the breathing to transform the Qi into Spirit. If the breathing is not refined, the Spirit will be insufficient, and the body will likewise be unhealthy. Serving only the Yin Spirit, the Yang Spirit cannot come into being.

Heavenly Spirit and Earthly Spirit

魂魄

Hun Po

The Heavenly Spirit is Yang; the Earthly Spirit is Yin.
The Before Heaven is Hun; the After Heaven is Po.
There are Three Hun and Seven Po.
When the Hun are ruling, the Po are controlled.
When the Po rule, the Hun are weakened.

The method consists of entering the stillness in meditation and using the Six Character Secret Transmission.[1]

Mentally produce the sound of *An* [唵] and sense it coming up through the navel so it can be fixed in the Middle Dan Tian. Then visualize circulating the Qi [at the Middle Dan Tian] to the left and right, each thirty-six times.

Mentally mobilize the sound *Ma* [嘛] and direct it to the liver, then revolve the Qi [around the liver] to the left and right each thirty-six times.

Mentally mobilize the sound *Nie* [嚙] and direct it to the heart. Revolve the Qi [around the heart] to the left and right each thirty-six times.

Mentally mobilize the sound *Ba* [叭], and direct it to the lungs, revolving the Qi [around the lungs] to the left and right thirty-six times each.

Mentally mobilize the sound *Mi* [咪] and direct it to the kidneys. Revolve the Qi [around the kidneys] to the left and right thirty-six times.

Mentally mobilize the sound *Hong* [吽] and extend it up to the Muddy Pellet, then revolve the Qi [around the Muddy Pellet] to the left and right each thirty-six times.

By concentrating the mind, the Hun Spirit [魂] and the Po Qi [魄氣, the energy of the Earthly Spirit] both revert to the highest point and are refined and transformed into Yang. Yin dwells in the Great Crucible [the womb]. Yin remains still and guards the embryo. Now, again, mentally mobilize the sound An and direct it to the Central Pass. After doing so nine times, the work will be complete. Yin rises and Yang descends, and they coalesce in the Central Crucible. A halo will encircle the

Book One: The Correct Course for Female Practice

Ultimate Gate [Muddy Pellet] just as it does with the Immortaless Guan Yin sitting atop Mount Potala.

---

1   The *Six Character Secret Transmission* is a semblance of the Six Healing Sounds. In the Healing Sounds, Xu (嘘) is used for the liver; He (呵) is for the heart; Si (呬) for the lungs; Chui (吹), the kidneys; Hu (呼), the spleen; and Xi (嘻) for the Triple Warmer.

Chapter Nine

Perfect and Illuminate the Yang Spirit

陽神完明

Yang Shen Wan Ming

When the Yang Spirit is pure, it becomes luminous and perfect, like the Immortaless Guan Yin sitting atop Mount Potala. When the conscious mind reverts to the Primordial Source, the Six Sense Desires are transcended and the Spirit becomes naturally perfect and clear. The virtuous daughter, Jade Maiden[1] of the Dragon King [王龍, Wang Long], holds a precious pearl in her hand, and as she offers it, light fills the ten directions. When the heart and kidneys have interacted, the Spirit and Qi naturally harmonize. The true seed is formed, and the divine embryo is nourished.

Purple Bamboos Separate means the nature of the liver is benevolent. The *White Parrot Dances as it Flies* means that the condition of the lungs is righteous. *Harmonizing Metal and Wood* means the temperament is unified. *Tiger Crouches, Dragon Descends* means the Water and Fire complement each other. The *Pure Precious Vase* is a metaphor expressing that the secretions of the lungs are pure. *Swaying Willow Branches* means the tail of the liver is in proper condition. The saliva of the *Flowery Pool* is comparable to Sweet Dew. The Muddy Pellet at the crown of the head sits unshakably as if atop Mount Potala.

> **Nine Revolutions and Seven Reversions**
>
> 九 轉 七 返
>
> Jiu Zhuan Qi Fan
>
> *The Nine Revolutions create the single drop of Yang Spirit.*
> *The Seven Reversions is the process of forging of Metal and Fire.*

The method of true salvation is to mentally produce the sound *An* and direct it to the place of the True Breath, the Great Crucible. Then the mind will be concentrated and all will be at peace. When the original Yang Qi is abundant and the fire of the spirit is bright and perfect, then the Great Medicine bursts through the Three Passes [also called Fields or Barriers] on the Front and the Three Passes on the Back.

One knows and contemplates only contentment. The heart is settled and the mind is pure. There is nothing but contemplation. This great method is the wondrous and profound True Secret, and is far superior to the method of Slaying the Dragon. Carry this out for Nine Revolutions and the Seven Returns[2] will be gained.

When the fruits of your practice revert to the navel, the Yang Spirit appears at the crown of the head. After the precious radiance has ascended, body and spirit both attain a wondrous state. One's meritorious achievement has reached perfection and the Heavenly Decree[3] is about to arrive.

Book One: The Correct Course for Female Practice

1. *Jade Maiden* (玉女, Yu Nu), also called Dragon Girl, is a Chinese deity. According to Daoist liturgy, she is an immortal-spiritual being who comes to the aid of those seeking immortality. As a disciple of Western Royal Mother (Xi Wangmu), her sexual Yin essence is an elixir of immortality—thus granting immortality to any male who invokes her properly either in the afterlife or in the present life.

2. See *Refining the Elixir: The Internal Alchemy Teachings of Daoist Immortal Zhang Sanfeng* (Valley Spirit Arts, forthcoming) for an explanation of the *Nine Revolutions* and the *Seven Returns*.

3. *The Heavenly Decree is about to arrive* means that the Heavenly Immortals/Officials will either have an immortal bestow a visitation upon a worthy mortal, or simply confer immortality upon the person.

Chapter Ten
Nourish the Yang Spirit
養陽神
Yang Yang Shen

When the Great Crucible is formed and the Great Medicine is obtained, the spirit embryo will manifest. Even though the Yang Spirit appears, it is still necessary to incubate the embryo. Nourish it for three years, and meditate facing the wall for nine years.[1] Refine the breath so it is gentle and continuous, give it undivided attention, and coordinate the spirit and breath. For three thousand days, guard it as if protecting an infant. Never forget this for an instant.

When the Yang Spirit is able to wander freely, the true self can travel comfortably at will. Even though still living in the world, great merit is established. When merit is fulfilled, the moment of destiny arrives and the true master appears [an immortal visitation], bestowing final salvation and bringing the new soon-to-be immortaless into the presence of the Exalted One [Lao Zi].

After this she visits all the Heavens and finally the Jade Pool to have an audience with the Golden Mother [Xi Wangmu] where she will receive her appointment as an immortaless, and so transcend the mortal world.

> ### Three Treasures
>
> ## 精 氣 神
>
> Jing Qi Shen
>
> *The Three Treasures are the medicines for curing mortality.*
> *Use tranquility to refine the Jing.*
> *Use harmonizing the breath to refine the Qi.*
> *Use Mind-Intent to awaken the Shen.*
> *With these three complete, you can soar as an immortal.*

Close the eyes for two days and light will follow wherever the mind draws its attention. Guard and hold it within the internal orifices [eyes, nose, mouth, and ears]. By entering tranquility the light will penetrate even deeper. The Qi will become warm like a springtime breeze and the Sweet Dew will flow profusely. The Qi will circulate throughout the body, starting at the womb and then coursing up the back and down the front. The River Cart turns of its own accord, transforming the mundane body into a true body. When a male realizes Yang Spirit, white light penetrates the crown of his head, and it will turn to black, to green, to red, and finally into golden light. When a female realizes Yang Spirit, black light will penetrate the crown of her head, and it will turn to white, then to red, to green, and finally into golden light.

When a person's cultivation is complete, the light will be perfected and the five lights unite as one. Earth-Thunder [in the lower abdomen] naturally resounds[2] and the Gate of Heaven naturally opens. The Yang Spirit goes forth and after doing so, returns. At first, the Spirit stays close by and later

Book One: The Correct Course for Female Practice

will venture out further. Be on guard against getting lost, for at this juncture, it is necessary to be very careful.

---

1   A reference to the cultivation practice of Bodhidharma, the founder of Chan (Zen) Buddhism in China, who entered a cave each day while residing at Shaolin Temple to meditate, doing so for nine years.

2   This can take several different forms in meditation practice. Some hear a loud bang, some the sound of thunder, some hear a cracking sound like an earthquake. In all cases this is an effect of ridding the body and mind of afflictions—i.e., "karma" for Buddhists and "transgressions" for Daoists. Primarily it means the cultivator has broken through the obstacles preventing them from obtaining true clarity and tranquility.

Book Two

張三豐仙人採真機要
Zhang San Feng Xian Ren Cai Zhen Ji Yao

The Immortal Zhang Sanfeng's Summary on Gathering the True Root-Power

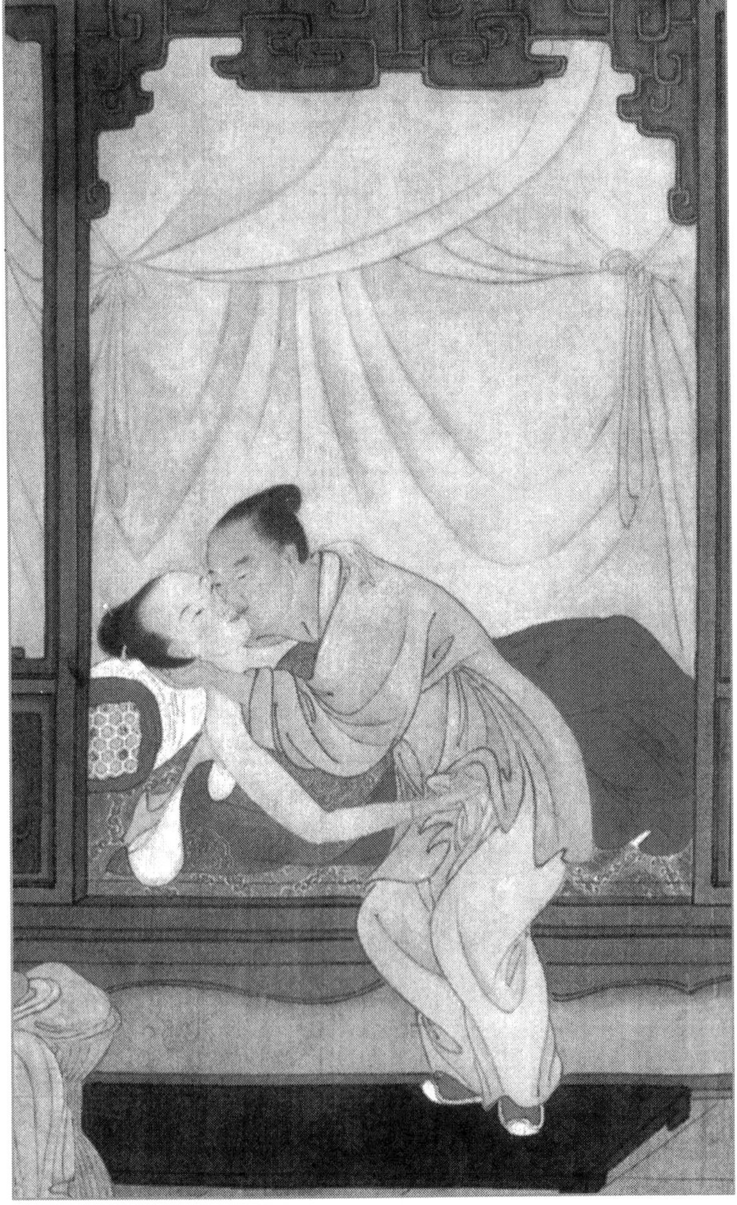

Part One

The Nine Fundamentals for Gathering the True Root-Power[1]

九基本採眞機

1   *True Root-Power* (機, Ji). The translation of *Ji* into English requires a twofold explanation: Ji means the mechanism by which all things are organically created, as well as the idea of it being the very pivot on which nature itself is balanced and supported. Hence, the idea then of Ji being the Root-Power and source from which all things operate in our world. Heaven has its Root-Power, Earth has a Root-Power, and Humankind has a Root-Power. In this text, Zhang Sanfeng is directing the idea of Ji as the True Root-Power in the context of Jing (primordial regenerative/sexual energy). By use of the term True (真, Zhen) the meaning goes to the Before Heaven condition of inherited Jing (innate, primordial, prenatal) source of Jing, not the After Heaven condition of acquired Jing (non-innate, temporal, postnatal) meaning.

Laying the Foundation[1]
築 基
Zhu Ji

My late teacher said, "There is Yin Breathing, Yang Breathing, Embryonic Breathing, and Closing the Breath.[2] Know the particulars of these [forms of breathing] and you can begin laying the foundation."

Laying the foundation is locking the Yin Jing[3] and entering the feminine. Maintaining the feminine without any internal vibration is to internally lock in the feminine energy securely. So, locking the Yin Jing is the goal for laying the foundation.

In laying the foundation, it is most important to maintain the feminine [a state of Yin] and not the masculine [state of Yang]. Maintaining the feminine is called "locking the Yin Jing." In this way it can be said with certainty that the foundation will be set up.

Alas! Did you not know? When the wind rises, the sail must be lowered, and when the jar is set upright the water will return fully to the jar.[4]

---

1 *Laying the foundation* is term for a beginning student of internal alchemy to practice breathing, meditation, developing heat (Qi) in the lower body (legs and abdomen), and training the concentration of the Spirit (神, Shen). From this *laying the foundation,* the work of internal alchemy can begin. Note that both treatises start with this principle.

Daoist Sexual Arts

2   *Yin* and *Yang Breathing* are both natural breathing methods. With *Yin Qi* (陰氣) the exhalation is longer than the inhalation. In Yang Qi (陽氣) the inhalation is longer than the exhalation. Both require an expansion of the abdomen when inhaling and a contraction when exhaling. *Embryonic Breathing* (胎氣, Tai Qi) occurs when the abdomen is contracted on the inhalation and expands on the exhalation. *Closing the Breath* (閉氣, Bi Qi) takes place after an inhalation and involves holding in the breath for a number of heartbeats before an exhalation takes place.

3   *Yin Jing* (閉陰精, Bi Yin Jing) translates as "Yin or female essence" or "feminine sexual energy." The term is applied to both genders, as males have Yin Jing just as females have Yang Jing (male essence). This follows the principle of *Yin within Yang,* and *Yang within Yin* (represented by the dots within the Taiji Symbol shown here). In Daoist internal alchemy the male uses the Yin to replenish his Yang, and females use the Yang to replenish their Yin. *Locking the Yin Jing* means to attain a level of tranquility (Yin) of both the body and sexual impulses. If an internal vibration is still occurring in the body during meditation, this means Yin Jing (tranquility) hasn't been achieved, and that the student shouldn't undertake the sexual alchemy practices until the vibration or shakiness ceases.

4   These aphorisms are revealing the process of reversal in internal alchemy, or as some texts call it, "the upside down." The common person is in a state of Yin/negative energy descent from birth, which gradually leads to death. The internal alchemist seeks to reverse this process by reversing the Yin into a Yang/positive energy ascent.

Fundamental One

Gathering the Medicine

採藥

Cai Yao

My late teacher said, "Lead is Jing [精], and the True Jing is what people inherit from their Before Heaven.[1] It is not the Jing of the After Heaven. Seek the Before Heaven Root-Power [先天機, Xian Tian Ji]."

When the foundation is securely locked, then one can study and practice to become an immortal. To attain immortality, the True Lead[2] must be found. When the True Lead has been gathered the foundation is locked.

The root source of this is in the Elixir Field.[3] So, if the True Mercury is dissipated, the True Lead cannot be sought. When one has acquired True Lead, then one can seek immortality; but, it is first necessary to set up the foundation and then go about Gathering the Medicine.[4] The medicine does not come just of itself, but solely depends upon your efforts.

Do not talk foolishly! When there is wine, what a pity guests are not invited. Without money how can one be a merchant?

1   *Before Heaven Jing* (先 天, Xian Tian), or *True Jing,* means the sexual energy people have in their youth, before it has been dissipated. In internal alchemy one of the main goals is to revert After Heaven Jing back to the condition of the Before Heaven Jing.

2   *True Lead* (眞 鉛, Zhen Qian) and *True Mercury* (眞 汞, Zhen Gong) and *Water* and *Fire* are pseudonyms for Jing and Qi. "Lead," "Water," and "Jing" are terms denoting the body, the nourishment of the body, semen/sexual secretions, saliva, bone marrow, tears, and blood. "Mercury," "Fire," and "Qi" denote the breath, energy of the body, heat of the body, and the emotions (Seven Po Spirits). Qi is the energy that animates Jing and body. Hence, the reference in the text on not dissipating the Mercury so the Lead can be sought, as with Qi moving the Jing, the Essences cannot be acquired. Again, the text points out the necessity of laying the foundation so the Qi can move the Jing.

3   *Elixir Field* (丹 田, Dan Tian) is the Qi center located about one inch behind the navel. It is the region where the internal alchemist concentrates the breath to develop True Mercury (Before Heaven Qi). Note that in acupuncture (the practice of Wai Dan, 外 丹, *External Elixir*) the Dan Tian is normally explained as being situated one inch behind and 1.3 inches down from the navel. In internal alchemy (Nei Dan, 內 丹, *Internal Elixir),* however, it is located one inch directly behind the navel, the area from which the umbilical cord was attached during gestation.

Book Two: Summary on Gathering the True Root-Power

4   *Gathering the Medicine* (採藥, Cai Yao) literally means to "harvest herbs." The term comes from *The Jade Emperor's Mind Seal Scripture* (玉皇心印經, Yu Huang Xin Yin Jing) wherein the context is about cultivating the Three Treasures of Jing, Qi, and Shen (essence, vitality, and spirit)—but here refers to them as herbs and hence the idea of medicines (藥, Yao). See *The Jade Emperor's Mind Seal Classic: The Taoist Guide to Health, Longevity, and Immortality* (Inner Traditions, 2003).

Fundamental Two

Knowing the Correct Time

知 正 時

Zhi Zheng Shi

My late teacher said, "Practice according to the Four Intervals as these are the correct times for acquiring Lead [Jing] and Mercury [Qi]."

The correct time must be known if the medicine is to be produced. Only after knowing this can East and West [Fire and Water] be matched. Before East and West are matched, it is difficult to produce the medicine. One must know the time when the medicine is to be produced.

Producing the medicine means to produce Lead. The medicine is produced at a specific time, and only if one knows the true time can one obtain the true medicine. Absorb your partner's Lead [Jing] to augment your Mercury [Qi].[1] When East and West are in a complementary union, the elixir is then naturally formed. Otherwise, one runs the risk of producing excessive Yin or excessive Yang.

Wait for the right time! The moon will come out and the Golden Flower[2] will appear. When the tide comes in, the water covers everything.

1   Another way in which to say, "Using the Yin to replenish the Yang," but in this case it is stating to use Jing (Water) to replenish Qi (Fire).

2   A reference to the teachings and text of *The Supreme One's Platform on the Mystery of the Golden Flower* (太乙金華宗旨, *Tai Yi Jin Hua Zong Zhi*), attributed to the Immortal Lu Dongbin (呂洞賓), also known as Lu Zu (呂祖). The term *Golden Flower* is interchangeable with the more common Daoist term *Golden Elixir* (金丹, Jin Dan).

Fundamental Three

Strumming the Zither

彈琴

Tan Qin

My late teacher said, "If the Dragon is not strong[1] how can he hope to play with the Tigress?"

The bamboo must be beaten until expanded,[2] and then the zither can be strummed. Strumming the zither and beating the bamboo produces the pure sound.[3] If the pure sound still has not yet arrived, the bamboo must be beaten again. Beat the bamboo until it expands, and then strum the zither.

"Beating the bamboo" clears the mind; "strumming the zither" excites the zither. I use my bamboo to excite my partner. When her zither is tuned, the "pure sound" will be loud and clear.[4]

Did you know? When the string is slack no arrow can fly. When the wind moves, one can then set the sail.

---

1 This is a comment directed at how a male must ensure he is sexually vital and able to produce strong erections to engage in the practices of sexual alchemy. If he is not sexually vital, due to his age or some debility, he must first undertake a regime of specific exercises, a disciplined approach to conserving Jing, and ingesting specific herbs to restore himself. See *Nine Jade Dragon Exercises* in the Appendix.

2   The *bamboo* (竹, zhu) is a metaphor for the penis and *beaten* is referring to self-stimulation to achieve a full erection in the event he is unable to immediately achieve an erection. *Beating the Bamboo* is also an action used for *strumming the zither* (琴, qin), the vagina, wherein the head of the penis is slid up and down between the labia until an erection is achieved. *Strum the zither* also refers to the use of the penis, tongue, or fingers to stimulate the vagina.

3   The *pure sound* (清音, qing yin) refers to the vocal expression a female makes when she is properly stimulated and is ready for penetration by the male. This "pure sound" is analogous to the sound of an arrow shot from a bow or the sound of a sail filling with air.

4   The idea here of the bamboo and zither producing pure sound is taken from the actions of a musician playing a zither. A large bamboo pick is used to strum across the strings of the zither. If this bamboo pick is not used correctly the sound produced will not be pleasant to the ear, but if used correctly the sound is pure and beautiful. Thus, the zither must be tuned properly and the bamboo pick must be used correctly in order for pure sound to be produced.

Fundamental Four

Approaching the Opposition

近 對

Jin Dui

My late teacher said, "It is such a pity the Dragon and Tigress do battle in the Hall of War. When seeing Falling Flowers the battle is over."[1]

In doing battle one must frustrate[2] the opponent. Though the opponent is aggravated, I do not play the hero.

If I do not renounce heroism, there will be contention.[3] In doing battle, the opposition needs to be aggravated first.

To do battle you must first approach the battlefield. I advise all you gentlemen, in approaching the battlefield do not underestimate the enemy. This expresses the idea that when having a sexual encounter, the male must allow his partner to take action of her own inclination, while refraining from initiating movement himself. If he were to move but once, he would lose his invaluable treasure.[4]

Cease thinking you should go wild! Cheating others is cheating yourself; losing to your own self is losing to others.

Daoist Sexual Arts

1   This opening verse is to be perceived internally and externally. The *Dragon* and *Tigress* (Tiger) are symbolic of the male and female sexual partners, as well as the two opposing natures within a person. The *Hall of War* is an analogy for the mind, and for the environment in which two people engage in sexual alchemy practice. In Chinese culture an old term for sexual activity, *Hua Yan* (華掩), roughly translates as "flowers and combat." The idea being that sexual intercourse can appear to be an act of love (flowers) and aggression (combat). In Daoism, the idea is to get rid of the more combative implications of sexual intercourse. Thus, only the more flowery aspects (Falling Flowers) of sexual intercourse are experienced. Also, this idea of seeing *Falling Flowers* is an allusion to a deep and abstract contemplative state (samadhi in Buddhism).

2   This is an implication of the male stimulating the female to a very high point of sexual stimulation, so she is in a state of aching for him to go further.

Book Two: Summary on Gathering the True Root-Power

3   The idea of *not playing the hero* means the male does not express unwanted or extreme expressions of masculinity. Doing so could create conditions of contention. It is far better in this situation for a male to let his partner be in charge of the activities and to request whatever expressions of masculinity she seeks from him. This is also a question of timing, as the male is expected to initiate the sexual activity, but once she is fully stimulated, he must take a more passive role. A Daoist analogy states, "The female is slow to heat, and the male is fast to burn." So following this idea of the male not taking on an aggressive role, like a proud hero, the female will have the necessary time to become stimulated and, likewise, prevent the male from dissipating too quickly.

4   If the male starts taking action, he will not be able to control his ejaculation, thus he would lose his invaluable treasure—his Jing.

Pan Gu (盤古)
Considered in Chinese mythology as the first being to come forth from chaos. Pan Gu is shown here preparing to invert Yin and Yang so to revert from mortality to immortality.

Fundamental Five

Inverting

倒

Dao

My late teacher said, "The secret of ending mortality is by reversing it. When we go in reverse[1] we are headed back to immortality, not towards death."

Carrying out the act upside down results in inversion. Only when upside down do the two things achieve completion. Completion depends on carrying out the act upside down.

Carrying out the act upside down results in inversion. "Upside down" means Earth over Heaven. Upside down means going against the normal course. The common method goes with the normal course, but the path of immortality lies in going against it. Following the normal course leads to the fire of suffering; going against it one becomes a Golden Immortal.

Upside down, upside down, only then is there completion.[2] You ought to know this! By her occupying the superior position, West has come to East.[3]

Daoist Sexual Arts

---

1   *Go in reverse* means going back to an infant's state of mind, wherein no thoughts of life and death disturb us. Most people live in fear of death, either consciously or unconsciously. This is because once the umbilical cord is cut, we are on a Yin descent through our life, and each moment we come closer to our end. The purpose of internal alchemy is to halt or prolong the Yin descent. Looking closely at the expected outcomes of internal alchemy, it is first about gaining optimum health, then increasing longevity, and finally, the ultimate goal, to obtain immortality, whether in the physical or spiritual sense.

2   This entire section represents the very heart of Daoist internal alchemy. Namely, *reversing, restoring, rejuvenating,* and *returning* —all of these are about going back, not forward. Looking closely at sexual internal alchemy it is easy to see that the male is attempting to get back to the youthful energy he had before masturbation took place, and as well to recreate the intense sensations he had when first ejaculating. For the female, it is about reducing her menstrual flow and recapturing her early sexual energy. In males the idea is to conserve their semen, yet regain increased sexual vitality. In females the idea is to increase their flow of secretions, yet reduce their menstrual flow. All of this can be seen as a *reversal* of the more common course.

3   *West* represents "water" and *East* represents "fire." Water is also "the female," and fire "the male." Therefore, the idea being presented here is that the female has come to a superior position over the male, as water in Daoism is considered the strongest of all the elements because it can overcome anything.

Fundamental Six

Utmost Sincerity

至 信

Zhi Xin

My late teacher said, "True sincerity means not being turned by conventions, rather you turn the conventions."[1]

So the desire to be immortal and for the True Lead requires utmost sincerity. Utmost sincerity requires that we use Mercury [Qi] for uniting with the Lead [Jing]. In the art of using the bedchamber, if in coming together one fails to truly converge, it is vain to hope for immortality.

The desire for immortality and the True Lead requires utmost sincerity.[2]

The desire for immortality refers to the heart's deepest hope. The True Lead is the Before Heaven Root-Power of True Qi. Desiring this Before Heaven Root-Power of True Qi to manifest in us requires absolute seriousness, extreme care, and utmost sincerity.

It is especially important that one mobilize a little of the True Mercury in the region within the anus [尾閭, Wei Lu][3] to welcome it. Moreover, this must be done just right.

Be careful! The Green Dragon must not seek the White Tiger, but the White Tiger herself must capture the Green Dragon.

Daoist Sexual Arts

---

1   This comes from a similar Buddhist verse, "Do not let conditions turn you, rather you turn conditions." In this text the idea is to not be turned by conventions, especially regarding sexual conventions. When engaging in sexual alchemy practices a person must sincerely engage in them and leave attitudes of romantic and self-pleasure behind. So you must let go of the normal conventions a common person adheres to when engaging in sexual activities. Males must let go of the ideas and actions of proving masculinity and employing selfish actions of ensuring their ejaculation, just as females have to let go of excessively expressing romance and bonding. Sexual alchemy, in order for it to be successful, must be approached as an equal partnership, and as a meditation focused on perceiving internal-spiritual awareness of both yourself and your partner. Again, it is about mindfulness, feeling, and awareness of the sensations, not becoming distracted by emotions and lust.

2   Absolute sincerity must be employed. If one's heart is not totally absorbed into the practices, then an efficacious response will not result. A Chan Buddhist adage runs, "The secret of attaining enlightenment rests solely in sincerity."

Book Two: Summary on Gathering the True Root-Power

3   Located about 2.5 inches on the upper part inside the anus is a gland and Qi center called the Wei Lu, or Tail Gateway (it is not just on the tip of the tailbone as its typically described). In Kundalini yoga this area is called the Kundalini gland. *Grey's Anatomy* refers to it as an "unknown gland," as its purpose was unknown to Western medical science. In this text, it is saying that the True Mercury (Before Heaven Qi) should be mobilized in the Wei Lu to stimulate this gland, which will then result in the Qi being able to ascend into the kidneys and up along the spine. The implication here is for anal sex, and a heightened focused attention, but with the warning that it must be done correctly and with caution, and equally that it must be the female who controls (captures) this activity. Again, as in so many aspects of these works, this stimulation can either occur from a physical act or through mental concentration on the area, as is done in seated internal alchemy.

小周天總圖

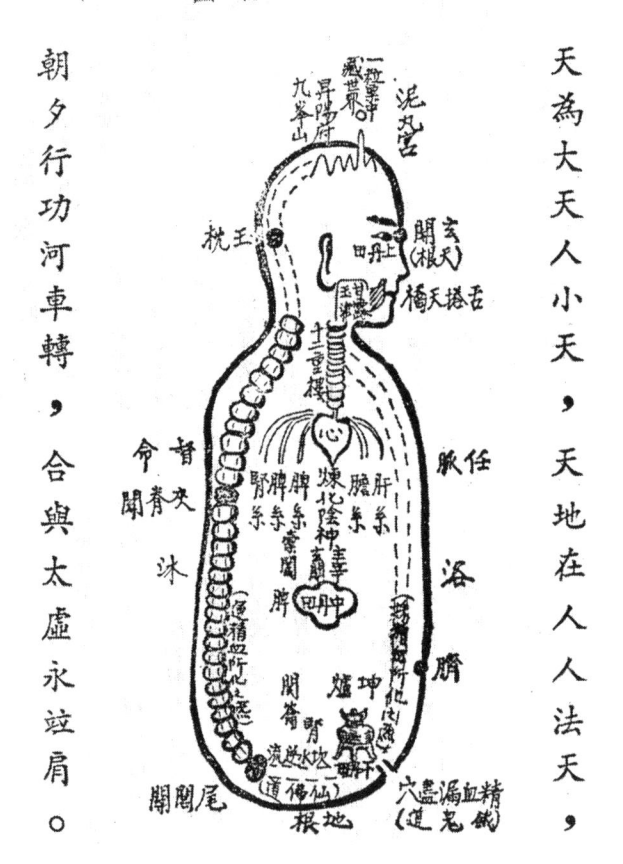

天為大天人小天，天地在人人法天，

朝夕行功河車轉，合與太虛永並肩。

河車周天

This image of the River Cart, here titled the Lesser Heavenly Circuit (Microcosmic Orbit), *comes from an internal alchemy document of the Dragon Gate Sect of Daoism.*

Fundamental Seven

The River Cart

河 車

He Che

My late teacher said, "When the Dragon is stimulated it will soar into Heaven." Capturing the Yang Jing is called "Acquiring the Lead." After obtaining the Lead, it immediately ascends to Heaven [the Ni Wan]. Having ascended to Heaven for a count of nine times nine.[1] It is securely captured. Capturing the Yang Jing is called "Acquiring the Lead."

"Capturing" means the Yang Jing cannot escape again. Yang Jing is the Before Heaven True Yi Qi,[2] the gold within water. To obtain this is to obtain the Lead. Carry out the practice of ascending in the back and descending in the front. Rising to the Ni Wan is called "Ascending to Heaven." After nine times of nine revolutions, the Golden Elixir naturally forms. A secret transmission is needed![3]

To ascend to Heaven, one must start to turn the wheel.[4] Only then can the Water rise.

---

1 *Yang Jing* is captured by bringing the *True Lead* (True Jing) up the spine into the Ni Wan eighty-one times. The True Jing is visualized up into the head by using Embryonic Breathing in stages of nine breaths nine times, and the visualization is seeing this True Lead as a fluid of golden color.

2   In *Before Heaven True Yi Qi* (先天眞一氣, Xian Tian Zhen Yi Qi) *Yi Qi* translates as "the one Qi," and carries the meaning of the "Dao of Before Heaven," or "Dao of the True."

3   Daoist texts often use cryptic statements to protect their teachings, hence the statement "A secret transmission is needed." In this text, the "secret" lies within the meaning of the Golden Elixir and how to begin turning the River Cart.

4   Two references to "wheels" appear in Daoist internal alchemy. One is to the *Navel Wheel* and the other, the *River Cart*. The Navel Wheel is about turning the Qi (heat/mercury) through the heart, spleen, lungs, liver, and kidneys and then bringing it down into the Wei Lu so it can begin its ascent up the spine. In Eight Brocades practice, this happens by visualizing a flame in the navel region—normally called the Fire Stage because it is about heating the breath and then mentally moving the heat through the Five Organs and into the Wei Lu. The *River Cart* is called such because the sensation of energy turning in the body feels like fluid, in contradistinction to sensations of heat. This is a result of cultivating the Jing that unites with the Qi. In Daoism, the art of cultivating the Jing primarily occurs through three practices: 1) *refining the Jade Secretion* (saliva), 2) *increasing blood circulation through disciplined breathing,* and 3) *retaining semen in males* and *reducing menses in females.* In *Refining the Elixir* (煉丹, Lian Dan), Zhang Sanfeng states that the separation of the Fire Stage into the Water Stage is like the sensation of feeling steam rising in the body. The steam condenses into water, which is then moved up the spine via the River Cart, just as a turbine wheel lifts water along its blades, or buckets, to power the grindstones in a mill.

Book Two: Summary on Gathering the True Root-Power

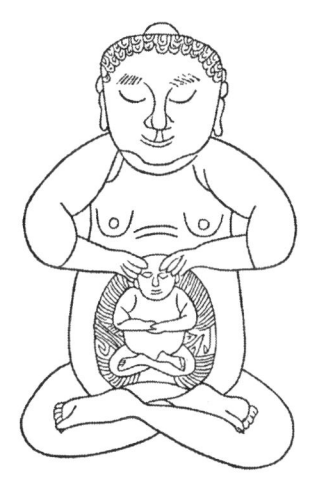

Image of the *Navel Wheel*.

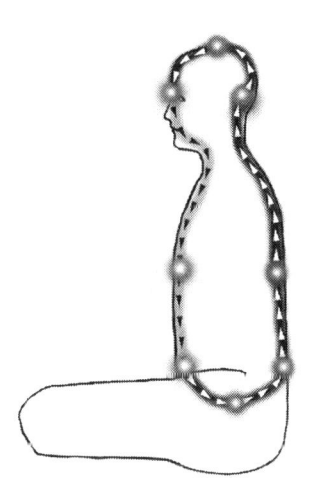

Image of the movement of the *River Cart*
(Lesser Heavenly Circuit).

Fundamental Eight

A Seal on the Gate

印 于 門

Yin Yu Men

My late teacher said, "When the head of the Dragon is full, put all your attention on the Ni Wan. Do not move. Let the Tigress seize the prey."[1]

The top of the head clearly bears a Seal on the Gate.[2] When the sign arrives at the fontanel, there is then perfect freedom.

There is also freedom when Water and Fire join in the head of the Dragon. The top of the head clearly bears a Seal on the Gate. You are the Dragon and the sign determines your stage of progress. When the tide reaches the highest point it is marked, so it is with the Gate.

The Qi of the "Red Water"[3] must traverse this gate and then descend. At this stage a stream of jade flows within the nose,[4] while on top of the head balances a Golden Pearl.

Daoist Sexual Arts

1. When the head of the penis feels very full this is a signal to put one's attention into the Ni Wan and let the female make all the movements. He should lie still and just focus on the fontanel area. The same is true for the female. When her areolae feel swollen and expanded, she should lie back and let the male make all the movement.

2. *Fu* (符) carries a broad meaning in Daoism. It can mean a "talisman," "tally," "seal," "charm," "mark," and "sign." The idea here is that when a cultivator experiences the elixir entering into the Ni Wan there will be an internal vision of it. This could be a bright golden pearl, a gold-white light filling the entire mind, a thousand golden lamps swaying gently, or even just a very pervasive sense of lightness, contentment, and joy. In all cases, the sensation is efficacious and profound. The meaning of the *Seal on the Gate* (符 門, Fu Men) is referring to the mind, which having had this experience is marked by it. In *The Jade Emperor's Mind Seal Scripture* when it states "one attainment is eternal attainment," it is referring to this *Seal on the Gate.*

3. *Red Water* (紅 水, Hong Shui) is a reference to blood. Most beginning internal alchemists think only of moving the Qi, but in actuality they should consider the circulation of the blood (an aspect of Jing) as well. Qi, in many regards, is like an inherent oxygen within the blood, so when the blood is well circulated, the Qi moves along with it.

Book Two: Summary on Gathering the True Root-Power

4   *A stream of jade flowing in the nose* is describing the effects of the descending elixir in the front of the body, which does produce mucus within the nose. Hence, when this mucus begins dripping from the nose, it is a sign of progress. This clearing of the nasal passage means the elixir can flow freely downward through the throat into the Mysterious Well (玄井, Xuan Jing, cavical area) and then down through the Bright Palace (明官, Ming Guan, solar plexus) and into the lower Dan Tian (behind the navel).

Fundamental Nine

Be With and Against the Natural Course

順 抗 自 道

Shun Kang Zi Dao

My late teacher said, "The male over the female causes *Adversity*; the female over the male brings *Peace*.[1] The Tigress only crouches to leap upward and the Dragon soars only to descend. This is being with and against the natural course of things."

Heaven over Earth will become Earth over Heaven. Only when Earth sits over Heaven can immortality be obtained. The immortal equals the longevity of Heaven and Earth. Heaven over Earth will become Earth over Heaven.

Heaven over Earth is called *Pi (Adversity)*. Earth over Heaven is called *Tai (Peacefulness)*. *Pi* represents the normal course, and *Tai* the reverse. The normal leads to mortality and the reverse to immortality. Without Earth situated above Heaven, how could one ever become an immortal? After attaining immortality, one's years are as long as Heaven's.

When you come face to face with this reality [of reversing Yin and Yang to oneness], Heaven and Earth are illuminated. Very few in the past or present have spoken of this.

1   These references are to two specific hexagrams in the *I Ching* (易經, Book of Changes). *Peacefulness* (泰, Tai) is the eleventh hexagram, and *Adversity* (否, Pi) is the twelfth. Here we see in #11, the female *Earth* trigram (Kun, 坤, upper three lines ☷) above the male *Heaven* trigram (Qian, 乾, lower three lines ☰). In #12, *Heaven* and *Earth* are in their normal mortal positioning.

#11, *Peace*	#12, *Adversity*
Earth over Heaven	Heaven over Earth

See *Book of Sun and Moon (I Ching),* volumes I and II (Valley Spirit Arts, 2014) for a full translation of the *I Ching* and how to use it for calculation and divination.

Summary of the Nine Fundamentals

九 基 本 總

Jiu Ji Ben Zong

Lock the Yin Jing and do not let it wander. Sit upright in meditation and after ten weeks, stop. Regulate sleeping, both in the night and day, and maintain your practice with constancy.

Freedom is won when the heart and kidneys interact. When the Qi and blood circulate everywhere there is a marvelous sensation. When body and spirit both reach this profound state, this is truly wonderful. The Jade Pillow [玉枕, Yu Zhen] and Muddy Pellet [泥丸, Ni Wan] transmit a message in the Void [虛, Xu]. While on both sides of the spine and through the Double Pass [雙關, Shuang Guan] the spring runs early.

It is most important to learn how to Close the Breath [閉氣, Bi Qi], and restrain it like completing a bowel movement [contract the anus]. In this way one begins to build the foundation. Now wait for the proper time and match the male and female.

The flute without holes must be held out straight. Simply blow into it so the Qi flows freely and cause it to fill with Jing, and so the wind naturally rises up into the Ni Wan at the crown of the head. For the purposes of "blowing the flute," practice with a female. Position yourself so to be opposite of each other. The instructions here call for a very sensuous woman [meaning, a female who is stimulated by oralism. If she isn't, the practice will be unfruitful].

The Record of Compounding the Elixir With Sexual Methods [性法合成丹記, *Xing Fa He Cheng Dan Ji*] states,
> If the flute is not blown, the Qi will not enter, and if the Qi does not enter, the path will not open. If the path is not open, the elixir will not pass. Because one cannot blow it oneself, one has a partner blow it, causing the path of Qi to open and the elixir to pass. Only then can it be refined. When you feel wind rising in the fontanel and Qi penetrating the Ni Wan, then this is the effect of "blowing the flute."

Part Two

The Seventeen Counsels on Gathering the True Root-Power
十七忠告採眞機

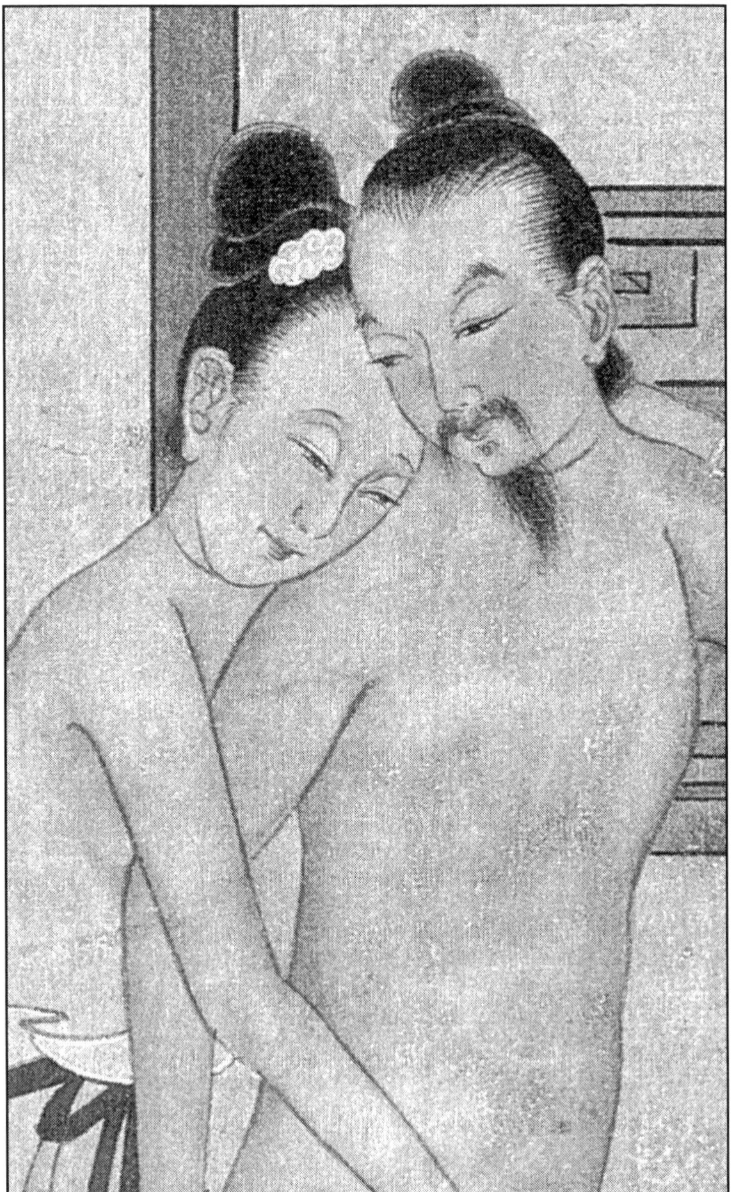

Counsel One

Strumming the Zither

彈琴

Tan Qin

Gently cupping her breasts together, entwining her thighs to stimulate her heart, and pressing into her to embrace her shoulders, then her true bliss is near. These actions produce the wondrous communication of a strummed zither, but there is no need to strum her zither with the fingers to produce the pure sound.[1]

Commentary by Zhang Zi

Strumming the zither means that the Dragonhead [glans penis] is placed near her lair [vagina]. The cupping of her breasts together and intertwining of her thighs excites her sensually. Pressing together and embracing her shoulders stimulates her true bliss. When she is sensually aroused, the pure sound comes; when true bliss is sensed the ultimate truth arrives. This is what is known as the pure sound that comes from within the stringless zither. Having obtained bliss from within the zither, why bother with the sound of the strings? Beating the bamboo causes my stem to dance; strumming the zither excites her lair. Having made my stem dance and having excited her lair, the pure sound comes forth naturally. Therefore, it is said if the pure sound has not yet arrived, one ought to beat the bamboo. When beating the bamboo opens up the lair, and the zither is well strummed, then this is no longer necessary.

When the string is slack, do not release the arrow; when the wind moves, the boat can be launched.

---

1   The whole idea of this method is purely preparatory. Both partners lie on their right sides. He cups her breasts together gently, places his left leg over her knee and then pulls his right heel back to be underneath her right calf so to appear to be intertwining her. He then lets his penis, the glans penis, gently move along her vagina between the labia. He continues this until she begins making sounds of pure bliss.

Counsel Two

Dragon and Tigress Intertwine
龍 虎 交
Long Hu Jiao

The Dragon first seizes the Tigress, and the Tigress seizes the Dragon. Dragon and Tigress entwine together, and the true bliss grows intense.[1] However, the methods handed down through the oral teachings and personal instruction must be applied. Through the oral teachings and personal instruction these principles must be faithfully carried out in the practice.

Commentary by Zhang Zi

When the Dragon and Tigress entwine together, the Dragon is on top and the Tigress below. This method is called "penetrating the stove" and "preparing the crucible." The Tigress uses her two arms to capture the Dragon, and the Dragon uses his two arms to seize her. This is precisely the coming together of the two "sevens" and the leaning together of the two partners. The previous chapter cannot compare with this. The oral transmission may be found in the next chapter.

1   The male moves to be on top of the female (missionary position) so he may enter her. There should be no forceful penetration. The male simply enters her deeply and remains in this position for the count of seven heart beats, then slowly withdraws his penis for a few moments and then enters her deeply again for seven heart beats. This is continued seven times in succession.

Counsel Three

Producing Fire, Stimulating Water
生 火 激 水

Sheng Huo Ji Shui

The oral transmissions must be passed from mouth to mouth,[1] and, relying on them, the mystery of the Way opens. When knowing how to issue Fire [Qi] and to penetrate the subtle light, then the Green Dragon can stimulate the profound Lead [Jing].

Commentary by Zhang Zi

In the art of the Dragon and Tigress it is taught that within the body the heart is ruler. The small intestines and tip of the tongue rule the heart, and therefore when tongue licks tongue, the Fire of the heart burns strong.

When the Fire of the heart burns strong, the small intestines are strengthened.

When the small intestines are strengthened, the Before Heaven True Lead is realized and about to arrive.

When the True Lead arrives, then the wonderful aphorisms of the oral transmissions and personal instructions will be realized.

1   The couple now focuses on kissing with the tips of their tongues. In the text, the character used for *Fire* is Qi (炁), not the normal ideogram of 氣, also pronounced Qi. In internal alchemy texts when the character 炁 is used, it is referring to the energy of the heat produced from correct breath and stimulation of the Jing.

Counsel Four

Green Dragon, Black Turtle

青 龍 黑 龜

Qing Long Hei Gui

When the Green Dragon appears, it stimulates the Black Turtle.[1] When a brilliant light flashes intensely, it penetrates the veil. If the head of the Green Dragon does not reveal itself, how could the Gate of Heaven open with the sound of Earthly Thunder?

> ### Commentary by Zhang Zi
> The Fire Dragon captures the Tigress. The Gate of Heaven is in the Northwest. Earthly Thunder [Earth over Thunder] is the hexagram *Fu (Returning)*. When one Yang is born in the Northwest, it is then the proper time for the Green Dragon to appear and excite the Black Turtle. This is known as, "When the one Yang begins to stir, then the mercury [Qi] leaks at midnight. Warm the lead [Jing] in the crucible and a brilliant light will penetrate the veil."

1. The *Black Turtle* is the female clitoris and G-Spot area in the vagina. It is called *black* because it is mysterious and hidden, and *turtle* because when a female becomes sexually stimulated the clitoris expands, like the head of turtle coming out from its shell. The mention of the *I Ching* image of *Fu (Returning)* shows one Yang line ascending through five Yin lines. It also represents *Thunder* (震, Zhen, the bottom three lines ☳) stimulating the female *Earth* (坤, Kun, the upper three lines ☷).

☷
☳

#24, Returning

In sexual alchemy terms, this image is showing the stimulation (Thunder) exciting the vagina (Earth). Thus, when the *Green Dragon* (penis) appears the *Black Turtle* (clitoris) is excited.

The reference to the Northwest is the direction location of Heaven (☰, Qian) in the After Heaven arrangement of the Eight Trigrams (八卦, Ba Gua).

Fire Dragon is a reference to Qi (Fire) and Yang (Dragon); meaning, the Yang Qi.

Counsel Five

The Dragon Appears to Seize the Tigress

龍 現 虎 拿

Long Xian Hu Na

When the Dragon reveals himself, he seizes the Tigress, and the two unite. Now is the moment for Earth to play the role of Heaven. Desiring to obtain this marvel, look to the role of reversal to see the mystery. The true secret arrives with the use of her tongue.[1]

Commentary by Zhang Zi

Earth is the Tigress and Heaven is the Dragon in reverse positions. "The Dragon reveals himself and seizes the Tigress" involves the methods for stimulating the partner. Whether upside down and downside up both express a longing for each other. Desiring the True Fire to reach the tip of the Dragonhead, it must be looked for through the true secret, beside and under the Tigress's tongue.

Continue to study the oral transmissions to obtain the pure sound. With Earth over Heaven there must be use of the tongue and heart. When Fire has been transformed into Water, it is time to begin. The Dragon occupies the Tigress's Cave, and the Tigress longs for the Dragon to enter. The Tigress stirs her tongue and the Dragon encourages her stirring. When the tongue is like fire, the tide runs. When it becomes like solid ice, Yang is born. This demonstrates the importance of practicing "Entering the Tigress's Cave."

---

1   This section makes references to oralism, with the female stimulating the head of his penis with her tongue, and the male stimulating her vagina with the tip of his tongue. In this oral practice the tongue is first made hot and sexual secretions are made to flow, but when the tongue becomes thickened and feeling more solid this is a sign that the Yang Jing is being produced.

Counsel Six

Dragon Enters the Tigress's Lair
龍入虎口
Long Ru Hu Kou[1]

When the Dragon dwells inside the Tigress's Lair, the intrinsic nature and sensuality are one. At this moment the Dragon must play dead. In the upside down position, the Tigress makes all the movements, and, after a short time, one drop [of Yang] arrives at my East.[2]

Commentary by Zhang Zi
"When the Dragon occupies the Tigress's Lair," this means the Dragon is on top and the Tigress is below The Dragon enters the Tigress's Gate. When the Tigress acts as guest of the Dragon, this is the same as the worldly method. When the Dragon acts as guest of the Tigress, this is the direction of the Dao. However, one must act dead to the world and be completely passive, allowing the partner to take the initiative, while we circulate the Yang Qi. If one does not carry out this kind of work, how can one expect to obtain that kind of transforming effect?

1   *Tigress's Lair* (Hu Kou) literally translates as the "Tiger's Mouth."

2   Here the text is explaining that during intercourse the male must act as guest by being on the bottom and with the female on top (Earth over Heaven), but he must remain motionless and let her take all the initiative regarding movement. This is the direction of the Dao because the female is taking an active Yang role and the male a passive Yin role—reversal.

Counsel Seven

True Lead Arrives

眞 鉛 來

Zhen Qian Lai

Although the Tigress's passion has become intense, the Dragon is oblivious. With trusting sincerity, she reveals her secret, as he waits for the right moment. When she lowers her head and closes her eyes, the True Lead has arrived. Over a long distance, it comes flying in like racing fire.[1]

Commentary by Zhang Zi

The Dragon asks the Tigress about her condition, for he is unable to know the level of her bliss. Only when he asks her does she tell him. If she "lowers her head and closes her eyes," the Dragon inhales through his nose and communicates with her on the mystery. Who can understand or comprehend this type of work? The effect is like seeing fire or a pearl.

1   When the male notices the female about to experience orgasm, signaled by her lowering her head and closing her eyes, he should inhale through the nose with a Reverse Breath, close the breath for twelve heartbeats, set the tip of the tongue up onto the upper palate, draw in the Wei Lu, roll the eyes upward as if to gaze internally at the Ni Wan, close the fists tightly, and sense her orgasm as best he can. When she orgasms, she inhales through the nose with Reverse Breathing, rolls her eyes upwards and puts her focus internally on the Ni Wan, draws in the Wei Lu, places the tip of the tongue up onto the upper palate, curls the toes, and imagines his penis rising into her solar plexus.

Counsel Eight

Eastern Road Opens

開 東 路

Kai Dong Lu

The White Tigress of the West receives the Green Dragon.[1] Unexpectedly, the Eastern Road is already open. After inhaling, do not let it return to the White Tigress. It would seem that this is all there is to the extraordinary art.

Commentary by Zhang Zi

The Tigress leaps, the Dragon dives deep, and again they turn upside down. The White Tigress receives the Green Dragon, and the Green Dragon receives the White Tigress. First, open the path through the back, and then inhale through the nose.

The Record of Compounding the Elixir With Sexual Methods states, "When the lead comes, it is like a 'pearl of fire,' and is used like a raft for ascending to Heaven."

Without the instructions from a master, how dare one recklessly embark? However, those who receive the true transmission all gain results without exception.

1 *White Tigress of the West* means when the vagina feels on fire she "receives the Green Dragon," and "the dragon dives deep" alludes to her taking his penis deep within her. The *Eastern Road* means her secretions are flowing. "After inhaling, do not let it return to the White Tigress" means that when he inhales, he imagines drawing in her secretions (True Lead) through the meatus of his penis directly into his Dan Tian. She then inhales and imagines drawing in his True Lead directly into her Bright Palace (solar plexus).

Counsel Nine

Push and Pull the Wei Lu

推挽尾閭

Tui Wan Wei Lu

When the East arrives, then push and pull. Failing to push and pull, it will leave the pass. If your practice is perfected, then naturally it will travel through the Wei Lu Pass.

Commentary by Zhang Zi

When the Tiger arrives, the Dragon points his feet toward Heaven and holding his two bent knees with his hands uses strength to "push and pull."[1] This passage involves more details than a Dragon tapestry.

If at this point there are additional discoveries, see above for matters of "refining the self." In reality, it is all here, including how to effect circulation of the whole body and achieve the marvel of swallowing [the Jing].

Daoist Sexual Arts

1   After the female has completed her orgasm and dismounts, the male places both hands behind his knees and pulls them towards his chest, inhaling when doing so with Reverse Breathing, and pointing his toes straight upward. When exhaling, he brings his hands around to the top of the knees and pushes them downward. When performing these "push and pull" motions, the male should feel some resistance in the legs so as not to feel that the movements are lax or too insubstantial. The male also feels that when pulling the knees up to his chest, his Wei Lu is being drawn in and affected by the movement. When exhaling and pushing the knees downward, he should feel as though the Wei Lu is being drawn up into the Essence Gate (精門, Jing Men)—the point between the two kidneys. All this should be repeated nine times. Regarding the statements about affecting the circulation and swallowing, this is a reference to the arts of the Lesser Heavenly Circuit and Refining the Jade Secretions. These may be found in the teachings and practices of the Eight Brocades Seated Qigong. Lesser Heavenly Circuit is about moving the Qi through the Du Mai and Ren Mai subtle meridians of the body, and Refining the Jade Secretion is about swallowing and refining the saliva.

Counsel Ten

The Doors of Qian and Kun

乾坤門

Qian Kun Men

Ordinary people firmly believe that the physical bodies of males and females are real, and yet think Water [坎, Kan] and Fire [離, Li] within them are false. Although the female's body belongs to Yin, her body becomes the male [Yang] body. The male belonging to Yang becomes the female [Yin] body. Do not be frightened here, the guest plays Qian, the host, for the male must teach himself to temporarily play the guest. Heaven, though above, turns over now to play the part of Kun.[1] Even though normally Kun is below, the Tigress reverses roles to play the part of Qian. When the partners alternate roles,[2] they are naturally joyful and adoring of each other. Yin and Yang must never be considered passive in their interactions. Even though feeling free in spirit and having contentment, one must be strictly conscientious. In this elegant and spotless house there must be mindfulness of expressing total sincerity.

Going in the gate, it must be delicate and with appropriate tact employed, and entering the door there should be a lingering and skill in waiting. Then at this time there is no danger and the conditions are favorable for the preservation of Yin and Yang.

Commentary by Zhang Zi

This is precisely the work of beginning the process. The completion of the act is a matter of man and woman. For the sake of discussion we consider them Kan and Li. I am fundamentally Yang, but contained within me is the Ultimate Yin; the Tigress is fundamentally Yin, but conceals within her the most marvelous True Root-Power of Yang. I take my body as a female's body and pretend that the female's body is a male's. The work is simply a matter of turning things upside down. Perfectly at ease, I guard my Jing, but am never idle and lazy about expressing it. Enter the hole in a leisurely way, withdraw with an attitude of sincere respect, and enter again slowly—but, whatever you do, do not be late in withdrawing.

---

1   Qian (乾), *Creativity of Heaven,* is the first hexagram in the *I Ching.* It is the strongest Yang image, representing the Heaven trigram ☰ doubled ䷀. Kun (坤), *Receptivity of Earth,* is the second hexagram. It is the strongest Yin image, representing the Earth trigram ☷ doubled ䷁.

Book Two: Summary on Gathering the True Root-Power

2. This role reversal is found throughout Asian practices dealing with internal alchemy. Even in Taijiquan a male student is taught to bring his body into a state of Yin, meditation itself is a Yin practice, and most Qigong practices are based on adhering to a Yin state. Whereas females come to these types of practices already Yin, so teachers have to encourage them to express more Yang energy. Within sexual internal alchemy both the male and female can learn to reverse their natural states of Yin and Yang. Females take the role of Yang, and males the role of Yin to replenish their natural state with the opposite so they can become completely balanced. It isn't that the male becomes female, nor the female becoming male. It is a matter of the female taking on a more Yang expression of energy, and males absorbing a more Yin-based energy.

Counsel Eleven

The River Cart

河 車

He Che

If the arrangements for this are questioned, the answer is that these are not difficult. The preparation work takes only a short time. The body reclines while the mind contemplates. The two knees are pulled up to the chest with the hands. This opens the path of the elixir, and prevents blockages. The River Cart rotates without allowing severance.

Ascend to Heaven with a count of nine times nine, do not be lax, and the energy will circulate through the passes.[1] Circulating and reverting, the path is long. Now quickly sit up straight in a pose of strength. It is essential that the buttocks contract as if restraining the bowels, and most importantly that the hands are placed alongside the waist. Inhale Qi through the nose to open the two pathways, White Tigress and Green Dragon, along the spine, and grit your teeth with the lips closed as you pull up the Yang and push down the Yin. If no strength is exerted, how can one expect the delicacy to enter one's mouth to taste?

Commentary by Zhang Zi

This is explaining that in the beginning when preparing to obtain the Lead [Water], the mind must contemplate and the body must be reclined. The hands "pull" the two knees until they press against the chest. "Ascending to Heaven for a count of nine times nine" allows the maintaining of the energy.

Capturing the Yang Jing is what is called "obtaining the lead." When I first obtain it I let out a laugh at her, and when she first attains it she lets out a laugh at me. When the elixir first appears, put all extraneous thoughts aside. The River Cart will move the stream with a remarkable power, powerfully raising it and maintaining a continuous flow.

"Ascend to Heaven" and Heaven will arise. Mobilize the River Cart and the water naturally circulates. When you realize the energy has made the turn, then quickly sit up straight. Now, maintaining a dignified demeanor, draw in the Wei Lu and place the hands on the waist so as not to let the energy move downward. If you want to "open the meridians along the spine" flare open the nose. If you want to "lift up Yin and Yang," raise the lower lip. When the elixir reaches up into the mouth, with confidence slowly and gently raise it up. When you experience these effects, clap your hands and laugh with a great "ha, ha!"

Book Two: Summary on Gathering the True Root-Power

1. The purpose of this section is to advise that when experiencing obtaining the Lead in the top of the head, one should sit in a cross-legged pose and seek to hold it there. The turn being spoken of here is when the energy gets to the top of the head in Ni Wan and then begins to descend. However, when first experiencing the energy in the Ni Wan it is best to hold it there and let it congeal before allowing it to descend. In many internal alchemy books, the rising of the energy up the spine into the Ni Wan is called "Advancing the Fire" and the descent is called "Yin Convergence." The entire circulation of the energy is called the "River Cart," or to say "the Lesser Heavenly Circuit." The point being is that it is best if the energy is first allowed to assimilate in the brain (Ni Wan) before allowing it to descend because the Mysterious Pass (玄關, Xuan Guan, Third Eye) needs to be stimulated and open before allowing the descent, otherwise the energy can be severed when it attempts to descend through the throat into the Mysterious Well.

Counsel Twelve

The Multistoried Pavilion

重樓軒

Chong Lou Xuan

When Lead [Water] arrives in the East, there is at first no awareness of it, but then one senses it entering like a rushing fire or pearl. Quickly revert the bodies, but taking care when withdrawing from her. Once having withdrawn the penis from her body, quickly commence with the work. Imagine the elixir really exists, and even though there is no substantial thing, pretend to raise it. Before raising it up, first know if the Mercury has arrived in the West [Fire].

When it comes to the East, quickly pull down the knees. Gently, nine times nine, and three times three, raise it up. Over and over, nine times nine, and three times three, elevate it. First, passing through the Wei Lu, it travels up the sides of the spine. Next, it approaches the Jade Pillow [玉枕, Yu Zhen] and then reaches the Ni Wan. When finally it has been transported to the Ni Wan Peak, how does it then descend through the Multistoried Pavilion? Swallow the saliva in the throat, repeatedly encouraging it to drop, as if pushing down on a scallion to plant it into the ground. Use the nose to temporarily draw it open. In a moment, without acting, it arrives at the mouth. In an instant, without moving, it naturally approaches the cheeks. It trickles down the throat to the Dan Tian, and with ten months of careful tending, the spirit embryo forms.

Commentary by Zhang Zi

When the meeting of Water and East takes place, carry out the method of "pounding the chest."[1] Afterwards, perform "Ascending to Heaven," quickly with the bent-leg exercise. Gently, nine times nine, pull it up in the front [of the body] and repeatedly, three times three, raise it in the rear [the back of the body].[2] Ah, who is capable of seeing it ascend? Only your self will know. It is easy to travel across water, but difficult to trek over a mountain peak, so it is with the crown of the head, the fontanel.

When you have gathered your partner's "sign," you must transport it to the gate and then send it down the "Multistoried Pavilion."[3] Therefore, it is said that even when it has reached the Ni Wan, this is not yet the Heavenly Bliss, but when it rests in the "Multistoried Pavilion," this is the joy of the immortals. Wishing to send it down to the Dan Tian, it must descend from the Ni Wan. When it travels to the Elixir Tally[4] then it naturally circulates to all nine orifices.

Now the "Jade Column"[5] flows in the nose and the "golden pearl" [金珠, Jin Zhu] balances on the fontanel. Entice and swallow the saliva down through the throat and feel as though the breath is being planted into the Dan Tian.

Now behold in the brain a gradual feeling of bliss. As the time approaches, it arrives at the mouth. Proceed with the utmost attention. Following its progression, do not move when it nears the cheeks.

Book Two: Summary on Gathering the True Root-Power

The work of gathering in the front only uses a moment of time, but advancing and withdrawing the fire and converging in the back requires an additional ten months.

---

1 Several new ideas of the internal process are being presented in this counsel. The first is the idea of "pounding the chest." This is done to ensure the breath and Qi descend from the upper chest. It is a safeguard method because in being sexually stimulated, the breath can get trapped in the upper lungs of males, so making a few pounding gestures upon the chest with the hands will drive the breath downward.

2 *Nine times nine* means to make eighty-one repetitions. *Nine* is the supreme Yang number, so making *nine repetitions of nine* is to complete the Yang energy within. Interestingly, Lao Zi's *Dao De Jing* consists of eighty-one chapters.

Three times three also equals nine, but here the *three* represents the Three Powers of Heaven, Earth, and Humanity.

In either usage, "to pull it up the front" is referring to the Three Passes on the front of the body, and to "raise it in the rear," means the Three Passes on the back. See p. 37 for the difference in locations of the "Three on the Front" for males and females.

3   The *Multistoried Pavilion* is referring to the throat and esophagus. Also called the "Twelve Storied Pavillon" or "Pagoda."

4   *Elixir Tally* (丹符, Dan Fu) is another name for the Dan Tian.

5   *Jade Column* (玉柱, Yu Zhu) is referring to the nose and nasal passage, as well as the mucus that will run from within it. When the internal alchemist, contemplative or sexual, opens the Ni Wan and the energy begins flowing downward (Yin Convergence), the nasal passage flares open and a very watery mucus will begin to slightly flow, just like with an infant.

Counsel Thirteen

Chun and Meng

純蒙

Chun Meng

Three Tigresses face the Dragon for the practice of irrigation. Always keep two Tigresses to act the roles of *Chun* and *Meng*. The two hexagrams *Chun* and *Meng* contain the words for forming the elixir through sexual alchemy. Put *Chun* and *Meng* to use morning and evening, for there must be protection against just one Tigress's monthly menses.[1]

Commentary by Zhang Zi

"Three Tigresses face the Dragon" means that while one Tigress has her menses, the other two play the roles of *Chun* [*Difficult Beginnings*] and *Meng* [*Youthful Folly*]. They have not yet had their periods and still possess their original Yang. In this way, the crucible rests on three legs. In the morning use this one and in the evening the other. When menses comes and the "flower opens," then again use the other. Begin with *Chun* and *Meng* and end with *Ji Ji* [*After Completion*] and *Wei Ji* [*Before Completion*].[2] After ten months, the fire is sufficient and the six hundred hexagrams complete.[3]

Daoist Sexual Arts

1   This particular counsel does not apply to our modern times nor our laws about engaging sexually with underaged persons. This practice was purely an expedient method and isn't necessary for the accomplishment of internal alchemy. A practicer of these arts could just as well use self-stimulation during the times when his partner is menstruating. We must not judge this counsel too harshly, however, as having multiple partners was an accepted and normal practice in Chinese culture. If legal-aged participants choose to engage in this practice, this is fine as well, but, again, it isn't necessary or essential.

2   The images referred to in this section serve as a symbolic reference to a virgin whose flower is opened (#3, *Difficult Beginnings*), and a developed young female who is unaware of the actual purpose of the practice (#4, *Youthful Folly*).

#3, *Difficult Beginnings*
Water (☵) over Thunder (☳)

#4 *Youthful Folly*
Mountain (☶) over Water (☵)

Images #64 and #63 represent the internal alchemical process of reverting Fire over Water to its opposite of Water over Fire.

#64, *Before Completion*
Fire (☲) over Water (☵)

#63, *After Completion*
Water (☵) over Fire (☲)

3   See the Sixteenth Counsel for Zhang's explanation of the "six hundred hexagrams."

Counsel Fourteen

Seek the Jade Flowers

玉 華 尋

Yu Hua Xun

Every month the red opens and every month arrives the gold. However, always prepare in advance to seize the gold. When the golden flower already has fallen, how can it compare to jade? When jade flowers are first born, this is the true scripture.[1]

> **Commentary by Zhang Zi**
> *When the time of gathering arrives,* this means to water and cultivate. The time of the creation of the medicine must be realized. Only knowing this can Water and Fire be united. Failing to realize it, there is then danger of the onset of menses. Observe the movement of the "tide" and the appearance of the golden flower. When the "tide" comes in, water overflows. Do not pluck the golden flower if already fallen, and pick instead the newborn jade bud. Both are sweet as spring water and congealed like an ointment. Observe the arrival of the menses, it is like the brightness of a clear full moon.
>
> Observe the roundness of the moon, as it is a sign of the coming of menses in the female. Although it is traceless and formless, you nevertheless must know and sense it.

Daoist Sexual Arts

1 The *red* is a reference to the menstrual flow and *gold* is a reference to the potent secretion a female can emit three days before her menses if she is properly stimulated. The text goes on to point out that if the female has already emitted her gold, then the male should seek it three days after the ending of her menses. The secretion, which tastes sweet and is thick in consistency, arrives from her *jade bud* (clitoris) being stimulated.

Three issues concern this *gold* reference:

First, the peak ovulation fluid is as restorative to males as semen is for females, and both in Daoism are considered medicines and elixirs.

Second, producing the "gold" is what benefits a female's health and longevity, and as long as she is producing it each month she can remain vital and youthful. This gold is the underlying reason why females in these practices seek to never be rid of their menses, just the reduction of it. In the case of menopausal females, they seek to restore it. As long as there exists the menses cycle, the gold cycle will continue as well. If the menses flow ceases, then so will the gold.

Third, this ovulation fluid is the basis for experiencing the Jade Pool Effect (see Appendix) in the vagina. When great quantities of it can be produced and developed into a thick, pure white substance, it is a sign of the True Jing being formed.

Counsel Fifteen

Obtain the Yellow Gold

得黃金

De Huang Jin

Now begin to understand how to seize your own life destiny, and the necessity of pursuing the process of watering and cultivating. From now on, continue to blow the flute without holes. Likewise, right away, pluck the stringless zither. When the zither strings become excited, withdraw into your own belly, and with fear and trepidation guard your heart. The myriad affairs of the world should all be put aside, and all of our thoughts should be concentrated on the yellow gold.

Commentary by Zhang Zi

It may not be said that, "Having obtained it, the work is done." After obtaining it, plant Mercury in the Lead Pond. From above, repeatedly cover it to stop the leaking and dripping. From below, repeatedly use the civil and the martial [Qi] to transmute it. Because this is carried out month after month, it is called "Watering and Cultivating." After ten months, take your leave of the crucible. It can then be observed that the method for cultivating the elixir requires a plan. Simply blowing the "flute without holes" is not wrong and simply strumming the "stringless zither" is not ignorance.[1] Follow the wind when the fire is being blown. Follow the water as though pushing a boat.

Keep it hidden in the abdomen, and be diligent every day. Guard it in the heart and be constantly cautious.

---

1   This counsel is about self-cultivation, not dual. Meaning, after ten months of practicing with a partner one embarks on solo meditation. Herein, the flute with no holes is referring to the idea of pinching off the meatus of the penis, and the stringless zither is referring to concentration upon the Gate of Life (命門, Ming Men).

Counsel Sixteen

Advancing Yang, Converging Yin
侯陽陰符
Hou Yang Yin Fu

From the beginning, the process of watering consists of six hundred divisions. Every division, each identical, consists of gathering the True Lead. At the hour of Zi, advance the Yang Fire by practicing the upside-down position. At the hour of Wu withdraw by Converging the Yin, turning it downside up. When it touches the Earth, then Wind produces Fire, and it seems to mount up the spine and descend the front of the body. Continue in this way for ten months and the work will be complete. Then face the wall and sit in a dignified manner for nine years.[1]

Commentary by Zhang Zi
The "process of watering" means incubating for ten months, or sometimes called "watering the infant." "Six hundred divisions" means every day employing the two hexagrams of Chun and Meng. In ten months there are three hundred days, so in the end we arrive at a total of six hundred hexagrams. One must perform Advancing the Fire at the hour of Zi, and Yin Convergence at the hour of Wu.

Now fire is born during the Earthly Branch Yin, and stored during the hour of Xu. Is it possible there is only the need to practice during Zi and Wu?

Between the morning and evening hours the methods of Yin and Yang are employed, never forgetting the technique of "upside down." Within the "living hours of Zi, Wu, Mao, and Yu" use the civil and martial fires [Qi] gently and subtly. Do not dare to make foolish interpretations, but wait for the master's instructions. Ha! Although most people in the world ridicule me, I chuckle at their ignorance.

This is the method of Twelve Dragons and Tigresses[2] having intercourse. First have the female "blow the flute" so the Qi enters and opens the Mysterious Pass. Then press her breasts together and entwine her thighs. Lean toward each other and embrace her shoulders. Excite her sensuality intensely. Alternate playing passive and aggressive. Using the tongue to suck tongue, stir up the fire in her heart and produce the flame of her desires.

When bliss is felt internally within her, and her whole face shines with a rosy glow, then she offers up her "pearl." Repeatedly excite her. When at last the One Yang is set in motion and the True Lead is about to arrive, then turn bottom over top, use tongue to lick the heart of tongue, and let the Dragon explore the Tigress's Cave.

Finally, when the Tigress's tongue is like ice and the Dragonhead is on fire have the Tigress carry out the movements. The Dragon, however, does not move. If it were to move, the Dragon could not overcome the Tigress in battle. Therefore, my late teacher said: "In doing battle, the Dragon must know how to allow the

Book Two: Summary on Gathering the True Root-Power

Tigress to be aggressive. While the Tigress is aggressive, the Dragon is not to attempt to play the hero."

When the Tigress becomes excited to the point she cannot contain herself, she is moved to her innermost part. As the "hour of the living Zi" arrives, she lowers her head and closes her eyes, and "sweet dew" fills her mouth. Now, when she probes the Dragon's mouth with her tongue, he inhales through the nose, causing the path of the spine to open.

Again, inhaling through the nose, the Lead comes racing like a Fire Pearl. The Jade Stem is warmed within the stove, and the Dragonhead is ablaze with fire. Now, with both feet facing Heaven, grasp the crooks of the knees with the hands, and using strength, pull them up and then push them down again until they are even with the chest.

At first, be gentle and later a bit stronger. Have her remove herself from contact with your body. Capture the True Lead as it soars through the Wei Lu.

Now quickly sit upright and contract the anus. Placing the hands on the waist, inhale through the nose, press the lips together, and gently raise it eighty-one times. Again, circulate it eighty-one times. When it travels through the Double Pass and Jade Pillow and reaches the Ni Wan, then quickly "plant scallions" with the nose,[3] swallow the mucus down through the Mysterious Well, and imagine that the brain produces secretions that reach the mouth, and then deliberately swallow it.

Daoist Sexual Arts

> When these two components [Jing and Qi] fuse in the Bright Palace [solar plexus], sit in meditation, and practice ascending and descending [Lesser Heavenly Circuit]; and then internalize the Jing and Qi by swallowing until Spirit and Qi merge.

---

1   The section provides a summary of the entire practice for *Gathering the True Root-Power.*

2   The name of this practice relates to the Twelve Earthly Branches, both the Yin and Yang aspects of them, with the Dragon being Yang and the Tiger, Yin. Therefore, it's noting a one-year practice period.

3   *Planting scallions* is a metaphor for closing off a nostril, and is normally called "Yin and Yang breathing." This is where a finger is used to close off one nostril (for example, the right side) and then breathing in through the open (left) nostril. Then that (left) nostril is closed off and the breath is exhaled and then inhaled through the opposite (right-side) nostril. The pattern then repeats by exhaling and then inhaling through the left-side nostril again, and so on. The idea is that the finger acts as a scallion being inserted (planted) into the nose to close it off, but the practice is really about pressing the finger against the sides of the nose to alternate the breathing through only one nostril at a time. The left-side breathing is Yang, and the right is Yin, hence the reason for calling this "Yin and Yang breathing."

Counsel Seventeen

The True Lead of Immortality

眞 鉛 仙

Zhen Qian Xian

Seeking immortality and the True Lead, there must be a striving for utmost sincerity, and with utmost sincerity welcome it with Mercury. If the two fail to meet, it is vain to hope for immortality. Seeking immortality and the True Lead, strive with utmost sincerity.

Commentary by Zhang Zi

The coursing of the Before Heaven True Lead through one's body is accomplished only by means of utmost sincerity. Because utmost sincerity is employed, one must mobilize a drop of True Mercury from the region of the anus to meet it. The time of the meeting must be precisely the right moment. If it is not the precise moment, it is useless to seek immortality. Be somewhat cautious! The Dragon should now refrain from seeking the White Tigress, while the Tigress seeks the Green Dragon herself. Gentlemen who pursue the True should first sit in meditation and regulate their breathing, circulate their Qi and lock the Jing to cause the Qi and blood to circulate throughout the body and the mind to be at peace.

Therefore, after perfecting the practice of breath retention, restraining the bowels, hoisting and pulling down [the knees], ascending and descending, and so forth for one hundred days in a secluded chamber, the passes and orifices will open. However, for the time being, do not be hasty.

Before one has carried out the gathering for 5,048 [days], first gather for thirty [Chinese] hours, using this to refine the heart, the intrinsic nature, the Jing-Qi, and the Immortal Sword;[1] to supplement the water, the fire, the bodily fluids, the Qi and blood; and to learn raising and lowering, transporting and lifting, and swallowing and sending. When all are operational, engage in the act at the proper time, Beating the Bamboo and Strumming the Zither. Harmonize one with the other, as Earth over Heaven commune after the fashion of the hexagram *Tai*. As the White Tigress's Tail moves and twists, the Green Dragonhead continually rises erect; as the Moon Cave closes and opens, the Heavenly Root is repeatedly excited. Because of the continuous closing of the Moon Cave, the Heavenly Root is constantly excited. Through constant excitation, the Wei Lu too will be repeatedly excited and thus repeatedly pinched tight. As the Wei Lu experiences this repeated pinching, the Sea of Jing cannot fail to be stimulated nor the Yin secretions fail to flow. It is almost as if one is inundated by a rising wave of pleasure, like swift waters against sand banks.

Now gnash and grind the teeth, stop the ears and close the eyes, shut the mouth, and inhale through the nose. Restrain the bowels and close the breath.

Book Two: Summary on Gathering the True Root-Power

Above and below, the gates are securely locked. Caress the Tigress's thighs, squeeze the Tigress's breasts, suck the Tigress's tongue, embrace the Tigress's waist, and plant the Tigress's knees upright. Pinch the Dragon's Door, advance the Dragon's Fire, use the Dragon's Will, and concentrate the Dragon's Mind.[2] Stimulate the Tigress's Lead and allow the Tigress to move, permit the Tigress to twist, and cause the Tigress to leak. When the Tigress's passion reaches the peak of intensity, the gold naturally floats up.

When the Tigress tightly embrace the Dragon's waist, when her head is lowered and her eyes closed, then the water already has descended. The Tigress's tongue is as cold as ice and the Sweet Dew bubbles forth like spring water. Now do not let her swallow it, but continually take it into your own mouth. When the Tigress's tongue is as hot as fire and the boiling water in the stove is scalding, then have her separate from your body and quickly withdraw your sword.

Return [to the supine position] with the feet straight up. Grasp the crooks of the knees and Ascend to Heaven for a count of nine times nine. The nose inhales and the tongue is sucked, the shoulders are raised so the Qi can be returned. Mobilize the consciousness and focus it in the Mysterious Gate. Keep the mind on the medicine. The head should be erect and the back straightened supporting it. As it passes through the Wei Lu, sit upright and place the hands on the waist. Inhale once through the nose and the medicine will rise up another level. It should be as if contracting the nose to punch a hole. At the same time, raise the back and it will naturally traverse the "Three Passes." Then with one pounding of the head and one pulling up of the lips, it will pass through the Jade Pillow.

Now, lower the head, and continuing to pull up the lips and "plant scallions" in the nose, it then naturally arrives at the Mud Ball in the crown of the head. Contract the nose and forcefully roar out in a downward direction. Then as though swallowing the saliva down the throat, first cause it to travel from the palate to fill the cheeks. Having transported this drop of "True Mercury," effortlessly and with a sincere heart and tranquil mind, send it down the "Multistoried Pavilion" to meet the "Golden Fluid" that was first swallowed.

When it reaches the "Middle Extreme," continue to sit in meditation, raising and lowering it. Breathe in the Qi and swallow the saliva, causing the spirit and Qi to fuse. From "Refining the Self" to the stage of "Watering and Cultivating," this is the one and only method. Only during periods of rest and withdrawing of the Yin Fu [陰符, Yin Convergence] does one stop temporarily. Carry out gentle cultivation and spiritual exercises, emphasizing attention to the minutest subtleties.

Those whose destiny it is to read these words will surely cultivate this secret virtue, and they will have no difficulty attaining the highest Dao.

Book Two: Summary on Gathering the True Root-Power

1. The *Immortal Sword* is a metaphor for an erect penis filled with Jing and Qi, or maybe better said, "An erection maintaining Fire and Water," along with the idea that there is no dissipation. Called "Immortal" because it is long lasting, and "Sword" because it can cut through the delusion of passion and the Six Sense Desires.

2. The *Dragon Door* is the meatus of the penis. *Dragon Fire* is the Yang Qi. *Dragon's Will* is the mind-intention, and *Dragon's Mind* means the conscious focus of using Yang energy.

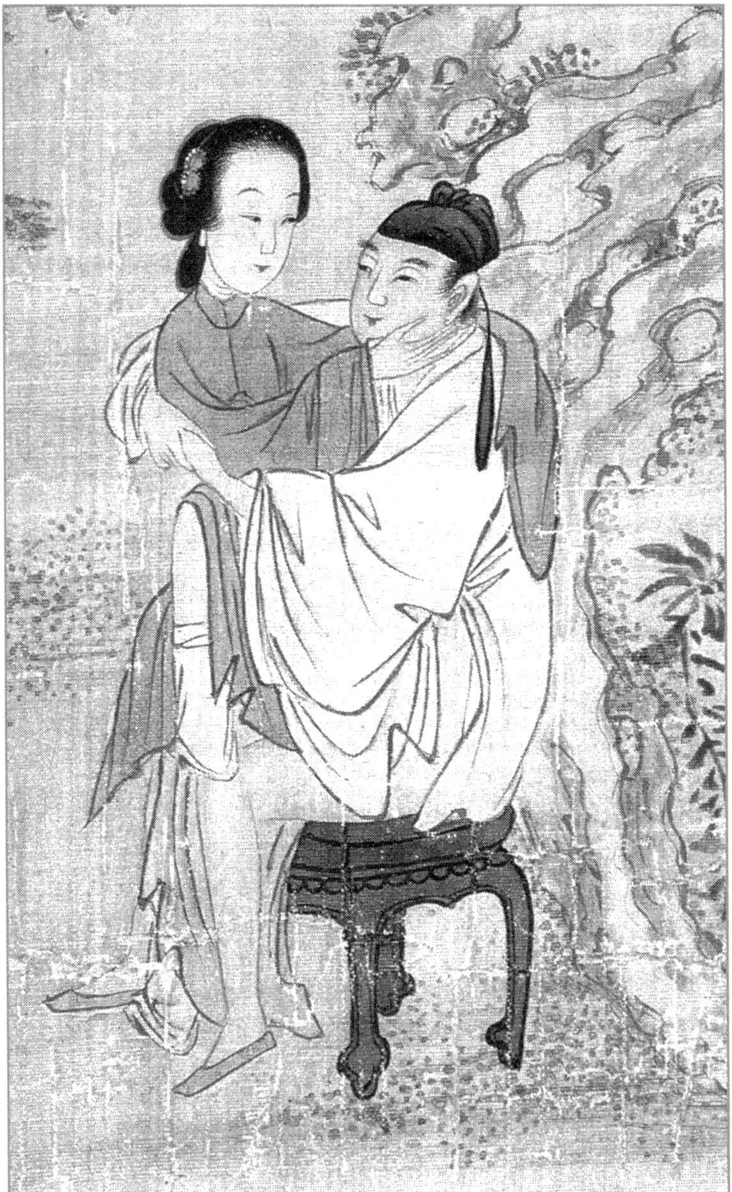

Appendix

This section provides a listing of recommended teachings for those who wish to engage in either the solo or partner practices of Daoist sexual arts.[1] The following practices are alluded to in the main texts of this work and so are presented here in greater detail.

Individual Practice Regimes for Restoration, Developing Jing, Accumulating Qi, and Illumining the Spirit

Eight Brocades Seated Qigong (for males and females)
八段錦坐氣功, Ba Duan Jin Zuo Qi Gong
Although it is practiced in many sects of Daoism, Eight Brocades is mainly found in the Perfect Realization Sect (全真派, Quan Zhen Pai), and is said to have been created by the first of the Eight Immortals, Zhongli Quan, in the Tang dynasty. These eight exercises develop Jing, Qi, and Shen, but are also the foundation for actualizing the sensation of the Lesser Heavenly Circuit, the flow of Jing and Qi through the extraordinary Qi meridians on the back (Du Mai) and front (Ren Mai) of the body.

Nine Jade Dragon Exercises (for males)
九玉龍行功法, Jiu Yu Long Xing Gong Fa
Deriving from the teachings of the White Tiger Green Dragon Sect (白虎青龍派, Bai Hu Qing Long Pai), these exercises are specifically for males. Created from the teachings that the Yellow Emperor received from Xi Wangmu (Western Royal Mother), these nine specific exercises for strengthening the penis include five supplemental exercises for harmonizing the Jing and increasing blood flow. This practice is enhanced with the use of herbal formulas and oil.

Nine Retentions Practice (for males)
九截止練習, Jiu Jie Zhi Lian Xi
Derived from the teachings in the *Plain Girl Classic*, this practice is designed to strengthen sexual vitality and enhance the health of the body and organs. Females can achieve the same benefits, but in their case, it is the practice of releasing nine orgasms, not restraining them.

Doe Exercises (for females)
麀活動, You Huo Dong
Deriving from the teachings of the White Tiger Green Dragon sect, these exercises were designed specifically for females. Sometimes called Healing Tigress (治虎女練習, Zhi Hu Nu Lian Xi), the practice includes Qigong methods for increasing sexual energy, reducing menstrual flow, restoring the breasts, tightening the vaginal opening, and increasing blood circulation.

Appendix

Tiger's Waist Qigong (for females and males)
虎腰氣功, Hu Yao Qi Gong
It's unclear which school in China first developed this practice, but it is found in many Daoist sects, such as in the hygiene practices of Wu Dang Shan (武當山, Matchless Warrior Mountain) and Hua Shan (華山, Flower Mountain). Also known as Swimming Dragon Qigong (游龍氣功, You Long Qi Gong), or Triple Bracelets Encircling the Moon (三環套月, San Huan Tao Yue), this popular Qigong exercise is used for slimming the waist, fortifying the kidneys, and strengthening the entire lymphatic system.

Hanging Tiger and Hanging Sea Tortoise Methods (for females and males)
吊龜法, Diao Gui Fa
See page 30 for more information. Although this practice is discussed in Book One for females, it can be beneficial for males as well.

Jade Stem Techniques (for females)
玉莖法, Yu Jing Fa
This method is derived from the Taboo Girl School[2] (某女派, Mou Nu Pai). The practice of the Jade Stem[3] involves using a facsimile of a penis carved from green jade. This "Jade Stem" is inserted into the vagina to not only stimulate sexual energy, but also for healing the body and inducing a more transcendental experience of spiritual-sexual awareness. This is a very powerful practice as its main time of use is during sleep and

therefore affects the subconscious mind. This practice should be approached carefully and preferably with guidance. It is one of the highest forms of sexual alchemy for females, as it relies on visualization techniques, Qigong breathing methods, and chanting.

Six Healing Sounds (for males and females)
六氣音, Liu Qi Yin
See page 70 for information on the *Six Character Secret Transmission* of healing sounds specifically for females. For information on the version of the Six Healing Sounds for males and females, see *The Immortal: True Accounts of the 250-Year-Old Man, Li Qingyun* by Yang Sen (Valley Spirit Arts, 2014).

Herbs (for females and males)
草, Cao
Certain herbs and herbal formulas both sexes should take not only enhance one's sexual vitality and health, but they also develop the Jing and Qi. Herbs are a crucial supplement to all Daoist practices and should not be overlooked.

Appendix

1   For more information on any of the practices described in this section, as well as forthcoming herbal products, please visit www.valleyspiritarts.com.

2   *The Taboo Girl School* supposedly began in the early Han dynasty, by whom is unknown. Taboo Girl (a name, and teaching, not to be revealed) was one of Xi Wangmu's four female attendants. See p. 13, note 1, for more information on Xi Wangmu and her other attendants.

3   *Jade Stem* is a term denoting the penis. Other systems have come to use a Jade Egg, predominately those of Japanese schools, but it is mainly used just for the stimulation of sexual energy.

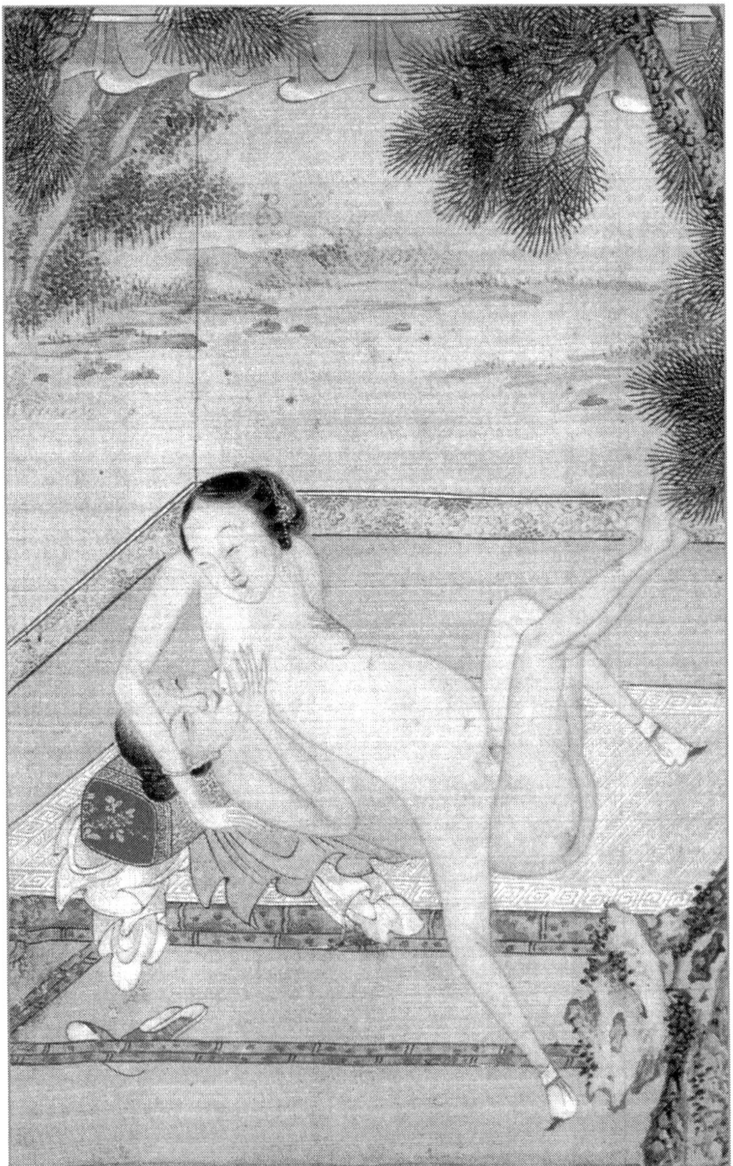

The Nine Sexual Intercourse Positions

九 性 交 姿 勢

Jiu Xing Jiao Zi Shi

Excerpted from the *Plain Girl Classic*.

The Yellow Emperor said to Plain Girl, "You have given me the specific knowledge for the correct approach and behaviors for sexual activity, which also entails using nine specific positions. Please enlighten me clearly on these, so that these treasures for practicing sexual activity may be recorded for my future reference, and so I can correctly practice these precious secrets of sexual joy." Plain Girl then detailed each sexual position for him:

The first position is called *Soaring Dragon*. With the female lying on her back with her legs raised upward and back towards her head, and the feet together, the male hovers over her from behind in a crouching fashion on his knees and begins rubbing his Jade Stem over her clitoral area. When the Jade Stem is fully erect he inserts it into her Jade Gate using the Eight Shallow and Two Deep method. When the erection reaches its peak and the feeling of the pending ejaculation is experienced, he withdraws his Jade Stem from her. When the sensation of ejaculation has subsided and the erection has softened slightly, he reinserts the Jade Stem and begins the Eight Shallow and Two Deep method again. He repeats this procedure ten times.

This technique will strengthen the Jade Stem and provide him with greater staying power, and the female will experience intense sexual pleasure from the contractions of her Jade Gate. This technique will also cure any stomach disorders either partner may be suffering from.

The second position is called *Forest Tigers*. The female lies face down with a pillow under her stomach to raise her buttocks. The male then positions himself on his knees behind her and holds her by the waist with both hands. He inserts the full length of his Jade Stem into her Jade Gate and proceeds to swiftly withdraw the entire length, repeating this movement of the Jade Stem thirty-six times. The male must prevent his ejaculation. After each set of thirty-six repetitions he rests until the Jade Stem softens slightly and there is no sensation of ejaculation, at which point he begins the technique again. He does this ten times in succession.

This technique will strengthen and eliminate any disorders the male might have of the heart and liver.

The third position is called *Playful Monkeys*. The female lies supine with a pillow underneath her to slightly raise her buttocks. She positions her thighs against her abdomen with the calves and feet raised straight up. The male, facing her, squats over her on

Appendix

his knees, with his Jade Stem positioned behind her buttocks. Using both hands he supports her legs on his shoulders so that her knees are positioned higher than her breasts.

The male then inserts the head of his Jade Stem into her Jade Gate and makes eight shallow thrusts. He withdraws the Jade Stem and slides the entire shaft twice along her labia and over the clitoris, as though making two deep thrusts. He then inserts the head of the Jade Stem, repeating this procedure ten times.

After the ten repetitions are complete, he inserts the Jade Stem even deeper into her [half the length of his penis] and repeats the same procedure another ten times. Finally, he inserts the full length of his Jade Stem and repeats the procedure ten times or until the female reaches orgasm.

This method will increase the hardness of erections and his staying power. It also strengthens the spirit and benefits longevity.

The fourth position is called *Mating Cicadas*. The female lies face down, with the legs held straight and together. The male squats over her and gently leans on her back while inserting his Jade Stem into her Jade Gate. She should attempt to raise her buttocks slightly to better feel the sensations of penetration upon the labia. He thrusts his Jade Stem into her fifty-four times.

During the male's thrusting, she alternates vaginal contractions with his thrusts and dilation during his retreats. After the fifty-four repetitions, he should rest momentarily, and then begin again. When the female reaches orgasm the procedure ends.

This technique will rid both of them of the seven emotional illnesses: depression, anger, sorrow, selfishness, remorse, fear, and nervousness.

The fifth position is called *Floating Tortoises*. The female lies on her back with her buttocks rolled up off the bed and her knees positioned up and over her breasts. The male kneels over her, drawing his body close to hers, and inserts his Jade Stem into her Jade Gate. With both hands he gently holds back her legs. With his Jade Stem he stimulates both the Jade Gate and her clitoris, inserting the Jade Stem, withdrawing it and letting it slide over her clitoral area, and inserting it again. He does this repeatedly until her secretions are flowing.

When the female begins grinding her pelvis from the intense stimulation of her Jade Gate, the male should then deeply thrust his Jade Stem into her and continue thrusting until she orgasms. He then stops.

This technique will make the male physically stronger and increase his vitality. It is also used for dispelling unwanted toxins in the five organs.

The sixth position is called *Flying Phoenixes*. The female lies on her back with her legs held apart and bent at the knees. The male kneels between her legs and supports his body by placing his forearms on the bed on either side of her. He inserts his Jade Stem deeply into her Jade Gate once, then withdraws it to slide back and forth across her vaginal area nine times. During the deep insertion of the Jade Stem the female should make short rhythmic and rocking movements to press the Jade Stem deep within her; she does this twenty-four times. This will cause her secretions to gush.

The female must be sure that she contracts her thighs around the male's waist when he has thrust his Jade Stem deeply within her, and relaxes the thighs when he has withdrawn and is stimulating the outside of her Jade Gate.

When she reaches orgasm the male will cease having intercourse with her. With frequent use of this method the Qi in the marrow of the bones will be benefitted.

The seventh position is called *Licking Rabbits*. The male lies upon his back with his legs together and straight out. The female mounts him, facing away from him, her knees bent and the legs held along the male's sides and under his shoulders. She places most of her weight on her knees and legs, supporting herself with her hands and arms, and allows her head to droop downward.

The male's Jade Stem is inserted deeply into her Jade Gate. She uses any motions of her choosing to stimulate herself and to cause her secretions to gush forth. When she orgasms, the intercourse is stopped. This technique will prevent the onset of illness.

The eighth position is called *Diving Fish*. The male lies on his back with his legs together and straight out. The female mounts him, sitting on top of his forelegs and facing him. Bending her knees with her legs extended out alongside his, she rests her weight on her knees and legs.

She then moves her buttocks forward, gradually allowing the head of his Jade Stem to enter her Jade Gate. Deep penetration is not allowed, however, and she must control the depth throughout. She uses any motion of her choosing to maintain shallow penetration, much like a baby just suckling upon the nipple, not engulfing the entire breast.

During this technique the male is to remain motionless and allow her to make the movements, which helps make the act of intercourse last longer. When she reaches orgasm, the Jade Stem is withdrawn. This exercise will prevent many types of ailments.

The ninth position is called *Crane Necking*. While facing the female, the male kneels with his knees held open and thighs spread apart. The female kneels in front of him with her thighs positioned on either side of his and her hands and arms placed around and behind his head.

Appendix

The male's Jade Stem is inserted into her Jade Gate, and the shaft will rub her labia and stimulate her clitoris. The male places both his hands on her buttocks to guide the up and down movements and to ensure penetration.

When the female orgasms, the intercourse is stopped. With this technique all Seven Traumas shall be eradicated.

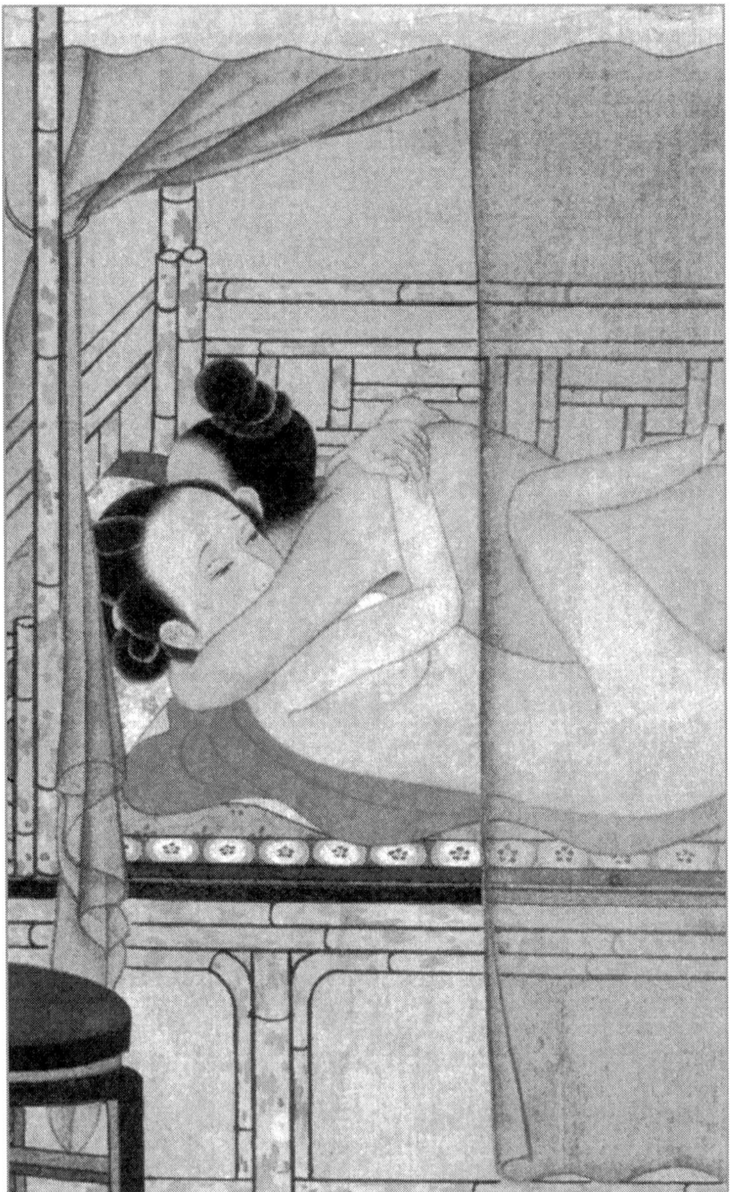

The Eight Benefits of Sexual Intercourse

性 交 八 利

Xing Jiao Ba Li

Excerpted from the *Plain Girl Classic.*

Plain Girl told the Yellow Emperor, "Sexual activity between a male and female can have both positive benefits and negative effects. If sexual activity is practiced in accord with balancing the Qi, diseases of the body and mind can be prevented and health can be maintained at its optimum. I will now explain the benefits and techniques."

The first technique is called *Strengthening the Jing.* The female lies on her right side with her legs stretched out and slightly bent at the knees. The male lies on his side in the same manner but with his head near her legs. They are lying opposite each other and facing one another's genitals. The male places his middle finger inside the female's Jade Gate and makes eighteen deep and rhythmic thrusts into her. The female places his Jade Stem in her mouth, and in unison with the male's thrusts she makes eighteen in-and-out deep sucking motions.

Doing this exercise two times per day for fifteen consecutive days will eliminate and prevent any abnormalities in the circulatory system. It will also thicken the male's semen and prevent the female from experiencing heavy menstrual periods.

The second method is called *Harmonizing the Qi*. The female lies on her back, supporting her head high up on a cushion, and spreads her legs wide. The male then kneels between her legs and supports himself with his hands and arms.

Just the head of the Jade Stem is placed inside the Jade Gate, and the male then makes twenty-seven slow and gentle thrusts. After this, intercourse ceases.

To ensure the efficacy of this method, it should be performed three times a day for twenty-one consecutive days. This technique rids the mind of all tension and regulates the pulses. It can also help cure frigidity in females.

The third technique is called *Accumulating Jing*. The female lies on her right side with the knees slightly bent and the buttocks protruding to the rear. The male lies on his right side directly behind her, placing his left hand on her left hip and waist.

The male then slides his Jade Stem through her closed legs and makes thirty-six thrusts against her labia. The female simultaneously stimulates the head of his Jade Stem with her left fingers. If Dragon Tears [龍泪, Long Lei, pre-ejaculation fluid] appear at the tip of his Jade Stem, she should retrieve the fluid with her left index finger and place it on her tongue for ingestion.

Practice this method four times a day for twenty consecutive days. This technique will strengthen a male's sexual energy so that it can be increased and developed in his body, thus creating a calm mind and

Appendix

relaxed body. In females, it cures and prevents frigidity. Keep in mind that ejaculation is not to occur.

The fourth method is called *Bone Marrow Strengthening*. The female lies on her right side, bringing her left knee up toward her chest and supporting it with both arms. She extends out the left leg and foot. The male hovers over her from behind, supporting himself on his knees and arms. He then inserts the head of his Jade Stem into her Jade Gate and performs forty-five slow rhythmic thrusts. When the thrusts are finished, the intercourse is over.

Practice this five times daily for ten consecutive days. This technique aids in strengthening the marrow of the bones and will help lubricate and keep pliable all the joints of the body. It will also encourage relaxation and mental stability and will help remove diseases in the body, especially chronic amenorrhea in the female.

The fifth technique is called *Harmonizing the Pulses*. The female lies on her right side, bringing her right knee up toward her chest and supporting it with both arms. She extends out the right leg and foot. The male hovers over her from behind, supporting himself on his hands and knees. He then inserts the head of his Jade Stem into her Jade Gate and performs fifty-four slow rhythmic thrusts. When the thrusting is finished intercourse is over.

Practice this six times daily for twenty consecutive days. This technique will regulate the male's pulses so they remain even and regular. In females the method will cure or prevent hyperkinesis.

The sixth method is called *Purifying the Blood*. The female and male kneel in front of each other, with the female's legs opened and positioned outside the male's legs, which are held together. The male holds her waist and hips with both hands, and she rests her hands upon his shoulders. His Jade Stem is inserted deeply into her Jade Gate. She makes thirty-six sensuous grinding motions with her hips and pelvis.

The male then lies back and the female bends over to place the head of his Jade Stem into her mouth, performing thirty-six complete circles around the head of his Jade Stem with her tongue. She simultaneously applies a tight and constant sucking action with her mouth.

The female then lies back with her knees held up near her breasts with her hands and arms, her legs and thighs held open. With the fingers of both hands the male opens her labia so that he can engulf her entire vaginal area with his mouth. He then performs forty-eight in-and-out sucking motions with his mouth.

To ensure the efficacy of this technique it must be performed seven times a day for ten days. This technique will greatly aid in stimulating the male's circulation, increasing the size of his glans penis, and

Appendix

strengthening his constitution. For the female, this technique helps her vagina to be more sensitive, increases her blood circulation, and prevents irregular menstruation.

The seventh method is called *Nourishing the Jing*. The female crouches down on her stomach with a large cushion placed under her so that her buttocks are raised high and her labia protrudes, allowing easy access for the male's Jade Stem. The male positions himself behind her, supporting himself on his hands and knees. He then proceeds to use the Nine Shallow and One Deep method in eight consecutive rounds.

To ensure efficacy of this method it must be performed eight times a day for ten consecutive days. This technique will strengthen the entire skeletal structure of both the male and female, and it will enrich their endocrine systems.

The eighth technique is called *Refining the Three Treasures*. The female lies on her back and draws up her legs with the knees bent and legs held together. The heels of her feet should be brought up to touch her buttocks. The palms of both her hands are placed firmly over her ears. The male kneels facing her and crouches over her with her knees pressing against his chest and his hands positioned on either side of her to support his weight. He then inserts the head of his Jade Stem into her Jade Gate and makes use of the

Nine Shallow and One Deep technique nine consecutive times. Then the intercourse is stopped.

This technique should be performed nine times a day for ten consecutive days. It will balance and enrich the Jing, Qi, and Shen of both partners, as well as cure any offensive vaginal odor in the female.

The Three Oral Treasures

三口交寶

San Kuo Jiao Bao

Derived and excerpted from the *White Tiger Green Dragon Teachings.*

The practice of the Three Oral Treasures includes three divisions with a Restoration, Transformation, and Celestial Method. Each of these methods are further divided into three stages of practice —including the Shen Stage, Qi Stage, and Jing Stage.

Below are the instructions for the First Division: Restoration Method. The second and third division methods, however, require the instruction of a qualified teacher, as they are quite powerful, hence the need for caution in learning them.

It is best to practice on the first and fifteenth auspicious days of the lunar calendar month. Seven days prior and seven days after a female's menstruation is also a good time to do this practice. Avoid practicing during the female's menstruation time, or if either partner is experiencing kidney problems. The Three Oral Treasures is not a daily practice. Wait at least one week between practice sessions.

Keep the practice room clean and fresh. If possible, use a room in which you do not have recreational sex. This helps you psychologically distinguish that this practice is different from your normal sexual routine.

Use a couch or bed for whoever is receiving to sit upon while the giver kneels on the floor between the other's legs. The receiver's torso should be reclined slightly yet propped up at no more than a 45-degree angle. The giver should be kneeling or seated in a cross-legged manner, facing the partner. Both partners should be comfortable and relaxed. Use pillows to prop up yourself or your partner.

When you start this practice, designate a certain amount of time to each part, such as ten minutes for the Shen, ten minutes for the Qi, and ten minutes for the Jing periods. Later these stages can be lengthened if so desired. Decide this with your partner beforehand.

Once the practice starts, talk sparingly. If you wish, use a timer—although this timer should be gentle so as not to startle you during practice.

As you become familiar with the practice, you should become increasingly mindful and eventually have no need for the timer. The time is not meant to be strict or rigid. Also, don't favor one section over another. Do your best to get through them all, giving each one the same amount of time and sincere focus.

Each of the three stages should be practiced so that each partner experiences receiving and giving nine times. If following

Appendix

the schedule of auspicious days (two per month), it will take nine months to complete the following method.

First Division: Restoration Method

Shen (神) Stage

There is no movement made in this stage of the practice for either person. Both simply breathe, sense, and concentrate.

Female Performing Fellatio (口淫, Kou Yin):

Shen method for the female giving:
> Place the penis in your mouth. It doesn't matter if it is erect or flaccid. Relax and focus on letting the breath sink and become steady. Sense the head of the penis. The penis should not be deep throated.

Shen method for the male receiving:
> Breathe naturally, keeping the breath steady and low. Refrain from wriggling and moving around. Place your hands along the sides of her head, but not on top, or place them over your Dan Tian.

Male Performing Cunnilingus (舔陰, Tian Yin)

Shen method for the male giving:
> Place your mouth gently and lightly over the female's vaginal area. Relax and focus on letting the breath sink and become steady.

Shen method for the female receiving:
> Breathe naturally, keeping the breath steady and low. Refrain from wriggling and moving around. Place your

hands along the sides of his head, but not on top, or position them to cup the breasts.

Qi (氣) Stage

Matched breathing should eventually start to happen. Do not try to match your partner's breath at first, just allow this to happen naturally. Movements in this section should be slow, steady, and controlled.

Female Performing Fellatio (口淫, Kou Yin):
Qi method for the female giving:
> The female's mouth slowly moves up and down the penis. The front of her tongue slides up the penis, and the backside of her tongue slides down the penis. She is inhaling up the shaft and exhaling when going down. While doing this she is visualizing a green mist coming out the penis and into her mouth as she inhales, filling her mind and body. When exhaling, she visualizes white Qi coming out of her and flowing back into his penis and body.

Qi method for the male receiving:
> Relax, breathe, and focus on the visualization, inhaling green mist and exhaling white Qi through the penis.

Male Performing Cunnilingus (舔陰, Tian Yin)
Qi Method for the male giving:
> The male's tongue moves up the clitoris on the inhale and down the clitoris on the exhale. The front of the

Appendix

tongue moves up the clitoris and the back of the tongue moves down.

Qi Method for the female receiving:
Relax, breathe, and focus on the visualization, inhaling green mist and exhaling white Qi through the vagina.

Jing (精) Stage

This section has the most movement; therefore, you must be focused on the fact that this is practice. It is easy to lose the practice and start to focus more on sexual satisfaction. *Don't let this turn into recreational sex.*

If during the first two sections the male feels like he is going to ejaculate, he should retain the ejaculation by closing his hands firmly into fists and using the Four Activities.[1] If he is unable to retain, stop the practice.

If the female feels she is going to orgasm during any of the stages, she should allow herself to do so freely, but she should retain the energy by using the Four Activities. During any of the stages, if she feels she is becoming exhausted she should let her partner know and they should stop.

Female Performing Fellatio (口 淫, Kou Yin):
Jing method for the female giving:
At this time you can practice stimulating the penis using any oral method. She should stimulate him up to the point of ejaculation and give him a chance to practice his retentions. While he is retaining, stop the stimulation.

You can hold the base of his penis and gently pinch the tip of the head to help him stop his ejaculation.

Jing method for the male receiving:
Practice the Nine Retentions if possible. If the female is able to stimulate you to the point right before ejaculation, retain the ejaculation by stopping the stimulation and doing the Four Activities. If you are able to do this nine times you will receive all the health benefits. If you are only able to retain a couple times, that's still beneficial. For the tenth retention, it is fine to ejaculate if you wish.

Male Performing Cunnilingus (舔陰, Tian Yin)
Jing method for the male giving:
Practice any oral method for stimulating her.

Jing method for the female receiving:
Focus on staying relaxed and breathing. Try not to move your body. If you orgasm, use the Four Activities to retain the orgasm. Whether you have orgasms or not you may need to let your partner know when you have had enough stimulation.

Appendix

1. The *Four Activities* involve internally gazing upward into the Ni Wan, placing the tongue on the roof of the mouth, drawing up the anal muscles, and inhaling to "close the breath" (meaning, to hold the breath for twelve heartbeats, or whatever is comfortable). This practice is found throughout Daoist internal practices. Here the intent is to Lock and Fuze. *Locking* means to retain the pending ejaculation, and *Fuzing* means to draw the energy up into the head so it fuzes with the Mysterious Pass (玄關, Xuan Guan, Third Eye), Muddy Pellet (尼丸, Ni Wan), and Jade Pillow (玉枕, Yu Zhen) Qi centers, thus creating an illumination effect.

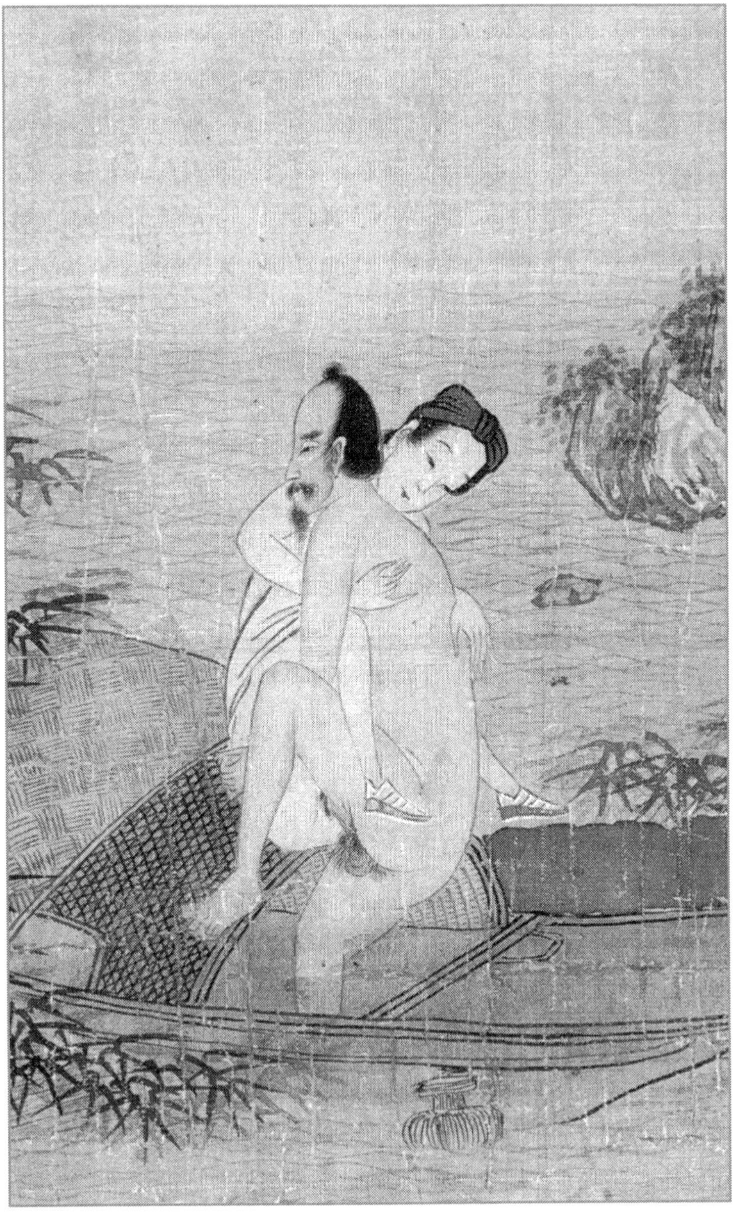

The Jade Pool Effect

玉 池 效 果

Yu Chi Xiao Guo

Derived and excerpted from the *Taboo Girl Transformation*
of the White Jade Immortaless Teachings.

In some cases, the term *Jade Pool* refers just to the mouth, but in other instances it refers to the extraordinary production of refined saliva in the mouth as well as the sexual secretions produced from the vagina. In Eight Brocades Seated Qigong, for example, the exercise called "Red Dragon Stirs the Sea" is a means for producing a large quantity of saliva in the mouth and then swallowing it down through the Ren Mai channel into the lower abdomen.

The saliva is heated through the swirling of the tongue over the teeth and gums (called Rinsing) and through sucking the saliva back and forth along the tongue (called Rousing). After which the saliva is divided into three parts and then swallowed down in three dramatic gulps and directed into the lower abdomen (the Elixir Field).

The goal of this exercise is to develop the saliva so that it becomes very thick and whitish in color, actually appearing the same as healthy semen or like the healthy secretions females emit during ovulation. This is not just the case of thickening and producing a very white substance, but it's also a means to produce extraordinary quantities of fluid. In essence, stimulating the salivary glands so an abundance of saliva is produced, similar

Daoist Sexual Arts

to the abundant drooling effect in infants. In infants, saliva is a necessary nutrition equal to that of breast milk, which is why infants produce such large quantities of saliva.

In Daoism, the purpose is far more than just absorbing nutrients, it is about creating the energies of Jing (Essence) and Qi (Vitality), but in this case it is the Primordial Jing and Qi (which were present in us before the umbilical cord was severed). In the Daoist practice of "living off Wind and Dew," the *Wind* represents the breath (Qi) and the *Dew* is refined saliva (Jing).

Saliva is one of the main components of Jing (along with blood, tears, sexual secretions, and other body fluids), but saliva is especially important because it can stimulate the production of what Daoism calls the "Three Peak Medicines." These secretions are produced from two cavities under the tongue, from two cavities under each breast nipple, and from one cavity beneath the clitoris in females, and from a cavity just beneath the frenulum on the backside of the penis (the sensitive area on the back upper side of the penis where the glans penis is parted).

These "medicines" can only be produced in conditions of high stimulation, euphoria, or transcendental states. The secretion in the mouth mixes in with the refined saliva (giving the saliva a sweet or honey-like taste). In brief, when this refined saliva and secretion is swallowed correctly it then stimulates the lower Elixir Field and intertwines with the heat of the breath (Qi). This produces what Daoists call "the elixir," which is none other than refined saliva, the medicine secretion, and the breath-Qi coming together in the lower abdomen (the Elixir Field).

The Jade Pool Effect in females can occur in the mouth and vagina. In males it is produced in the mouth as well, and through

Appendix

developing an extraordinary abundance of semen. The production of saliva in the mouth, however, is the most effective for benefitting a person's health and longevity, but beyond that, refined and replenished saliva is a component of the elixir of immortality and so, therefore, must be cultivated properly to aid in the process of creating the elixir. This can be accomplished through specific oral sex methods or by practicing Red Dragon Stirs the Sea.

Partner practices may develop the Jade Pool Effect sooner than the individual exercise of Red Dragon Stirs the Sea, but in any event, when it does occur, it is absolutely necessary to find a knowledgeable teacher who can instruct you on how it should be developed and used for internal alchemy.

Just producing the Jade Pool Effect can have wondrous benefits for a person's health and longevity, and if you can take the teachings further, the internal alchemy aspect can transform and immortalize your spirit.

About the Translator

Stuart Alve Olson, longtime protégé of Master T.T. Liang (1900–2002), is a teacher, translator, and writer on Daoist philosophy, health, and internal arts. Since his early twenties, he has studied and practiced Daoism and Chinese Buddhism.

As of 2015, Stuart has published more than twenty books, many of which now appear in several foreign-language editions.

Biography

On Christmas Day, 1979, Stuart took Triple Refuge with Chan Master Hsuan Hua, receiving the disciple name Kuo Ao. In 1981, he participated in the meditation sessions and sutra lectures given by Dainin Katagiri Roshi at the Minnesota Center for Zen Meditation. In late 1981, he began living with Master Liang, studying Taijiquan, Daoism, Praying Mantis kung fu, and Chinese language under his tutelage.

In the spring of 1982 through 1984, Stuart undertook a two-year Buddhist bowing pilgrimage, "Nine Steps, One Bow." Traveling along state and county roads during the spring, summer, and autumn months, starting from the Minnesota Zen Meditation Center in Minneapolis and ending at the border of Nebraska. During the winter months he stayed at Liang's home and bowed in his garage.

After Stuart's pilgrimage, he returned to Liang's home to continue studying with him. He and Master Liang then started traveling throughout the United States teaching Taijiquan to numerous groups, and continued to do so for nearly a decade.

In 1986, Stuart published his first four books on Taijiquan—*Wind Sweeps Away the Plum Blossoms*, *Cultivating the Ch'i*, *T'ai Chi Sword, Sabre & Staff*, and *Imagination Becomes Reality*.

In 1987, Stuart made his first of several trips to China, Taiwan, and Hong Kong. On subsequent trips, he studied massage in Taipei and taught Taijiquan in Taiwan and Hong Kong.

In 1989, he and Master Liang moved to Los Angeles, where Stuart studied Chinese language and continued his Taijiquan studies.

In early 1992, Stuart made his first trip to Indonesia, where he was able to briefly study with the kung-fu and healing master Oei Kung Wei. He also taught Taijiquan there to many large groups.

In 1993, he organized the Institute of Internal Arts in St. Paul, Minnesota, and brought Master Liang back from California to teach there.

In 2005, Stuart was prominently featured in the British Taijiquan documentary *Embracing the Tiger*.

In 2006, he formed Valley Spirit Arts with his longtime student Patrick Gross in Phoenix, Arizona.

In 2010, he began teaching for the Sanctuary of Dao and writing for its blog and newsletter.

In 2012, Stuart received the IMOS Journal Reader's Choice Award for "Best Author on Qigong."

Daoism Books

- *The Immortal: True Accounts of the 250-Year-Old Man, Li Qingyun* by Yang Sen (Valley Spirit Arts, 2014).
- *Book of Sun and Moon (I Ching),* volumes I and II (Valley Spirit Arts, 2014).
- *Being Daoist: The Way of Drifting with the Current* (Valley Spirit Arts, 2014)
- *The Jade Emperor's Mind Seal Classic: The Taoist Guide to Health, Longevity, and Immortality* (Inner Traditions, 2003).
- *Tao of No Stress: Three Simple Paths* (Healing Arts Press, 2002).
- *Qigong Teachings of a Taoist Immortal: The Eight Essential Exercises of Master Li Ching-Yun* (Healing Arts Press, 2002).

  Forthcoming
  - *Clarity and Tranquility: A Daoist Guide on the Meditation Practice of Tranquil Sitting.*
  - *Refining the Elixir: The Internal Alchemy Teachings of Daoist Immortal Zhang Sanfeng* (Daoist Immortal Three Peaks Zhang Series).
  - *Seen and Unseen: A Daoist Guide for the Meditation Practice of Inner Contemplation.*
  - *The Yellow Emperor's Yin Convergence Scripture.*
  - *The Actions and Retribution Treatise.*

Taijiquan Books
Chen Kung Series
- *Tai Ji Qi: Fundamentals of Qigong, Meditation, and Internal Alchemy,* vol. 1 (Valley Spirit Arts, 2013).
- *Tai Ji Jin: Discourses on Intrinsic Energies for Mastery of Self-Defense Skills,* vol. 2 (Valley Spirit Arts, 2013).
- *Tai Ji Tui Shou: Mastering the Eight Styles and Four Skills of Sensing Hands,* vol. 4 (Valley Spirit Arts, 2014).
- *Tai Ji Bing Shu: Discourses on the Taijiquan Weapon Arts of Sword, Saber, and Staff,* vol. 6 (Valley Spirit Arts, 2014).

Forthcoming Books in Chen Kung Series
- *Tai Ji Quan: Practice and Applications of the 105-Posture Solo Form,* vol. 3.
- *Tai Ji San Shou & Da Lu: Mastering the Two-Person Application Skills,* vol. 5.
- *Tai Ji Wen: The Principles and Theories for Mastering Taijiquan,* vol. 7.

- *Tai Ji Quan Treatise: Attributed to the Song Dynasty Daoist Priest Zhang Sanfeng,* Daoist Immortal Three Peaks Zhang Series (Valley Spirit Arts, 2011).
- *Imagination Becomes Reality: 150-Posture Taijiquan of Master T.T. Liang* (Valley Spirit Arts, 2011).
- *The Wind Sweeps Away the Plum Blossoms: Yang Style Taijiquan Staff and Spear Techniques* (Valley Spirit Arts, 2011).
- *Steal My Art: The Life and Times of Tai Chi Master T.T. Liang* (North Atlantic Books, 2002).
- *T'ai Chi According to the I Ching—Embodying the Principles of the Book of Changes* (Healing Arts Press, 2002).
- *T'ai Chi for Kids: Move with the Animals,* illustrated by Gregory Crawford (Bear Cub Books, 2001).

Kung Fu Books
- *The Eighteen Lohan Skills: Traditional Shaolin Temple Kung Fu Training Methods* (Valley Spirit Arts, 2015).
- *The Complete Guide to Northern Praying Mantis Kung Fu* (Blue Snake Books, 2010).

Downloadable Audio Recordings
(Exclusively through the Valley Spirit Arts website)
- *Setting Up the Foundation* (Instructional Recordings). Includes instructions on the different breathing techniques used for stimulating the Qi for completion of the Lesser Heavenly Circuit. Details on understanding the stages of Three in Front, Three on the Back; 36 and 24 Breaths; and Realizing the Dan Tian are given.
- *Daoist Sexual Arts for Health, Youthfulness, Longevity, and Spirit* (Seminar Recordings). The recordings of these three classes provide useful information on how to apply sexual energy and methods for restoring and revitalizing your quality of life. Health begins with acquiring sexual vitality and accumulating Qi. These audio recordings will give you the necessary tools for accomplishing both. Companion course to the book *Daoist Sexual Arts*. Includes three PDFs of Stuart Olson's translations on the "Rosy Clouds" chapter from *The Immortal*, selected works from *The Plain Girl Classic*, and sections on *Harmonizing the Yin and Yang*.
- *Yellow Court Scripture* (Course Recordings). The information in these 70 audio recordings is simply not attainable anywhere else. Recorded from online classes that Stuart conducted with a student over a year and a half, this commentary on the *Yellow Court Scripture* touches on Daoist philosophy, meditation,

internal alchemy, medical Qigong, and the spirit world like no other Daoist material provides.

DVDs
- *Li Qingyun's Eight Brocades* (Valley Spirit Arts, 2014). Companion DVD to the book *The Immortal.*
- *Eight Brocades Seated Qigong Exercises* (Valley Spirit Arts, 2012). Companion DVD to the book *Qigong Teachings of a Taoist Immortal.*
- *Wind & Dew* (Valley Spirit Arts, 2012). This version of Wind & Dew was designed to work in conjunction with the Eight Brocades DVD (also the Li Qingyun version). All three DVDs also work with the teachings in the Setting Up the Foundation Audio Recordings.
- *Taiji Qigong* (Valley Spirit Arts, 2013). Companion DVD to the book *Tai Ji Qi.*
- *Master T.T. Liang's 150-Posture Yang Style T'ai Chi Ch'uan Form* (Valley Spirit Arts, 2014).
- *Master T.T. Liang Taijiquan Demonstrations* (Valley Spirit Arts, 2014).
- *Tai Ji Quan Self-Defense Instructional Program* (3-DVD Set) (Valley Spirit Arts, 2011).
- *Healing Tigress Exercises* (Valley Spirit Arts, 2011).
- *Tiger's Waist: Daoist Qigong Restoration* (Valley Spirit Arts, 2009).

Visit the Shop at Valley Spirit Arts for more information:
www.valleyspiritarts.com/shop/

Also check out Stuart's author page at Amazon:
www.amazon.com/author/stuartalveolson

About the Publisher

Valley Spirit Arts offers books and DVDs on Daoism, Taijiquan, and meditation practices primarily from author Stuart Alve Olson, longtime student of Master T.T. Liang and translator of many Daoist-related works.

Its website provides teachings on meditation and Internal Alchemy, Taijiquan, Qigong, and Kung Fu through workshops, private and group classes, and online courses and consulting.

For more information as well as updates on Stuart Alve Olson's upcoming projects and events, please visit: www.valleyspiritarts.com.

About the Sanctuary of Dao

Established in 2010, the Sanctuary of Dao is a nonprofit organization dedicated to the sharing of Daoist philosophy and practices through online resources, yearly meditation retreats, and community educational programs. The underlying mission of the Sanctuary of Dao is to bring greater health, longevity, and contentment to its members and everyone it serves.

Please visit www.sanctuaryofdao.org for more information about the organization and its programs.

Made in the USA
Charleston, SC
02 May 2016